School of Evangelism
Training Manual

School of Evangelism
Training Manual

David W. Hopewell, Sr., D.Min.
Founder

The Joshua Ministry
School of Evangelism

David Hopewell, Sr., D. Min.

This manual is designed for the purpose of training and engaging leaders who will train others. The course offers strategies and principles that will help churches create strong evangelism ministries and believers for effective evangelism work. The course will also identify those things that keep congregations chained to the pews and offer solutions to break those chains, so we can begin to fulfill the Great Commission.

Joshua Ministry School of Evangelism
Table of Contents

The History of the Joshua Ministry

The Joshua Ministry story began in the 1997 after I accepted a ministry position at Greenforest Community Baptist Church in Decatur, Georgia, under the leadership of the late Dr. George O. McCalep, Jr. The evangelism strategy and principles during that time were based on several chapters in the Book of Joshua. These Scriptures give us a strategy for evangelism, and offer step-by-step principles for successfully possessing our land through evangelism. In 2001, *The Joshua Ministry, God's Witnessing Army* book was published, which contains the principles and a strategy for evangelism based on unity. Eight years and four publications later, I realize the thrust of my call and writings promote our efforts to work together. God has directed my steps in developing me personally and the Joshua Ministry.

In 2004, the book Keys to Becoming an Effective Associate Minister & Church Leader, which promotes the development of associates and unity with their pastors, was published. Recently we have authored an associate minister training manual.

In over thirty years of ministry, God has allowed me to serve pastors in the area of training associates and in the area of church growth and evangelism. He has allowed me to gain experience as I served twelve years as the Minister of Evangelism at Greenforest Community Baptist Church in Decatur, GA.

He has also developed me as I served as a consultant for the Atlanta Baptist Association helping churches develop strategies to effectively reach their communities. God has allowed me to serve on committees for the North American Mission Board of the Southern Baptist Organization, strategizing and developing evangelism material, *The Net*, an evangelism strategy for the 21st century. He has also privileged me to work as a contract worker with the North America Mission Board, where my responsibilities include training and developing evangelism strategies for African American churches.

Currently I am an Adjunct Professor at Beulah Heights University in Atlanta, Georgia, where I teach Urban Evangelism and Leadership.

My training, circumstances, events, experiences, and most of all the direction from the Lord, has inspired me to launch Joshua Ministry Inc., The Joshua Ministry School of Evangelism, and Joshua Ministry School of Associate Minister Training.

My sincere prayer is that the biblical principles, personal experiences, and knowledge conveyed in this manual will help in your personal development and inspire you to be all God is calling you to be.

HOW TO USE THIS MANUAL

The 12 sessions may be presented in one of several ways. Choose the option that best suits the needs of your congregation or group.

Option #1: Twelve Weekly Sessions
Sessions are scheduled for 2 hours each. Class time may be less than 2 hours, based on material and class participation. However, the presentation of class material will take approximately 90 minutes, based on the teaching style of the presenter. The practicum may take more than 2 hours.

Option #2: Weekend Modular
Sessions are scheduled for 2 hours. Sessions are held Fridays and Saturdays. Sessions are scheduled for 2 hours long but may be reduced to 90 minutes if the material can be disseminated by the instructor.

Option #3: Weekends
Sessions are scheduled on 2 consecutive weekends. Sessions are held Fridays and Saturdays. Sessions are scheduled for 2 hours long, but may be reduced to 90 minutes if the material can be disseminated by the instructor.

INTRODUCTION

The door of our churches swing wide with parishioners seeking to worship the Lord in spirit and truth, but very few parishioners leave from those same doors and enter the fields, which are ready for harvest. The questions is: How can we experience God's presence during a service filled with praise, worship, and a life-changing word, then leave out of those same doors of the church, get into our cars, and drive by fields ready to be harvested? Likewise, how can we go through our normal everyday routine, allowing perhaps hundreds of persons to pass us by daily, but never once communicate the gospel message to a lost friend, neighbor, loved one, or stranger? Does God's power only move us into a posture of praise and worship, but not into the fields of harvest?

This manual provides a complete, step-by-step process from the call of the Great Commission, praying effectively for the lost, sharing a testimony, and presenting the gospel. In the last section, we give recommendations for follow-up and discipleship.

For Best Results

Before implementation, I suggest the following. First, churches spend a period of time in repentance, seeking God, petition for the lost and celebration for the harvest.

Repentance

If we are going to experience the power of God in revival, repentance must occur before our evangelism efforts. Individual and corporate sins must be acknowledged and confessed. Most sins we commit are known; however, some might be unknown to us.

For example, on several occasions I have spoken with lost persons or members of churches who have shared stories of prejudice toward members and lost persons based on socio-economic status, educational background, gender, race, and class. In one case an usher refused to allow a prostitute entrance because she was a prostitute. In another, members actually cursed at visiting young inner-city boys saying, "Pull up your so and so pants." The boys left vowing never to return. One was shot in the head and killed. Maybe he would have been somewhere else doing something different, who knows. In a separate case, teens from an apartment complex began to visit the church next door. I received a call in which I was asked, "How should our church handle the following problem? We have teens coming over from the apartment complex next door, and we don't want them here. Believe me, I have more stories. Are we preventing others from entering into the kingdom (Matt. 23:13)? The religious sect of the day refused others entrance into the kingdom.

Perhaps we are standing in the way of sinners (Ps. 1:1). We do this when we are prejudiced towards others based on their race, gender, or class. Christ extended love to us when we did not deserve it. Jesus loves, accepts, and values us. Question: Should we not demonstrate the same to others?

Further, we hinder our witness when we demonstrate a fragmented body to the world. We do this when we treat others who believe salvation exclusively through Jesus Christ as enemies. Our actions are because they are part of a different denomination. If the body of Christ is fragmented and in need of healing, how then can we bring healing to others when we need healing ourselves? I believe when we come together in unity, it will witness to the world that Jesus is the Christ. Read more in my book, *Unity, the Highest Form of Evangelism.*

Are we hindering our witness to others when we lack a genuine authentic witness? Do we turn away sinners? When we live in hypocrisy, we hinder others from coming into the kingdom. Why should a person receive Christ if they can attend church and continue to live the same lifestyle? I have had that question posed to me by sinners. In fact, I posed that question myself before I asked Christ into my life. When we live as the world we are living in hypocrisy and hinder our witness to the world. I believe we will produce a greater witness to the world when we practice what we preach!

Leader, lead participants in the following prayer:

"Heavenly Father, I have sinned and am guilty of prejudice and/or have been standing in the way of sinners. Please forgive me. I do not want to hinder your work or stand in the way of someone receiving salvation through your son, Jesus. Forgive me. In Jesus' name, amen."

Seeking God

Sample prayer: "God, we are seeking your direction in this process. You may want us to make an adjustment or start in a specific neighborhood or member. We want to make sure we are sensitive to the Holy Spirit's leading."

Petition for the Lost

During this time, we intercede for lost family members, neighbors, co-workers, and loved-ones. During this time we also ask God to empower us for service.

Celebration

Members celebrate by praising God for the harvest He is going to give. Praise Him for chains of bondage being broken. Praise God for setting the captives free.

Notes

WHAT EVERY STUDENT NEEDS TO KNOW ABOUT EVANGELISM

The Great Commission is the instruction of our resurrected Lord Jesus Christ to his disciples, that they spread his teachings and make disciples of all the nations.

I want to stress the importance of making "disciples." We can make a convert but we have not fulfilled the Great Commission until we have made a disciple.

The work and the mission of the church is the Great Commission. The commission is not optional or something that needs to be prayed about, relative to ones involvement. Why pray about something God has commanded you?

We are to go into all the world and make disciples of all nations. The most famous version of the Great Commission is in Matthew 28:18–20, but also found in other gospels. Being sent by Jesus as the Father has sent him (John 20:21), going to Jerusalem, Judea, Samaria, and to the ends of the earth (Acts 1:8), preaching repentance and remissions of sins (Luke 24:47–48), signs shall follow us (Mark 16:15–17), and that He would be with us until the end (Matthew 28:20). We are to reach all peoples. If we only reach those of our own persuasion, we segregate the gospel.

Who's Responsible for Carrying out the Commission?

This may seem like a very simple question. However, it is one of great confusion and misunderstanding among many Christians. The confusion centers around Ephesians 4 text. The confusion is based on the roles of those who function in the office of the five-fold ministry. It seems that most view the role of the evangelist as the one who is responsible for carrying out the Great Commission. However, this passage designates leaders that train others to carry out the work of ministry (Ephesians 4:11–14).

All Christians are called and are responsible for carrying out the Great Commission. Based on the Scripture passage found in 2 Corinthians 5:17–21, we receive a ministry at the time of the new birth. The ministry is called the ministry of reconciliation, which means we are to unite lost men and women back to God. We are given this ministry or assignment at the time of the new birth (1 Corinthians 5:17). This passage makes all Christians responsible for fulfilling the command of Jesus. This passage makes all of us evangelists!

The second misunderstanding is that among some within the Body of Christ, the evangelist is not recognized, or his or her functions are to travel from one church to another and preach. Not to minimize the work done, just to mention that the role of the evangelist includes leaving the walls of the church.

Most Christians view the Ephesians passage as a select group of individuals. They and they alone carry out the work of the Great Commission because they have been called as evangelists. We preach and teach evangelism from the pulpit with little or no response. Could it be that congregants do not respond because they believe the message is for the called evangelist or those who have the "gift" of evangelism, or function in that office according to the Ephesians passage above?

No, we are all called. This perception only hinders our effectiveness and our ability to mount up a mass army of trained witnesses.

Mission vs. Evangelism

This is another area of confusion among some. There even seems to be tension among those in both camps. Is the Great Commission missions or evangelism? We are all on the same team seeking to fulfill one commission. I find both terms within the commissions. Go into the entire world, the Great Commission, making disciples, evangelism.

We must be careful however. You can go on missions without evangelizing, but you can't evangelize without being on mission. You can do all the good and help people all over the world but never mention Jesus and extend an invitation to someone to be a disciple of Christ. We need to do both to fulfill the Great Commission.

Types of Evangelism

I have listed some twenty types of evangelism. Those of us who have a passion for evangelism understand and compartmentalize evangelism for clarity, specialize training, and perhaps as a means of attacking some who would respond for specific training of interest. For training purposes and simplicity, let's be simplistic about evangelism.

1. The commission, mentioned above.

2. Types of evangelism, listed below, describe the type of evangelism, targeted group of people, and setting. Example: type: door-to-door evangelism; Target group: youth; setting: urban.

3. Evangelism is as simple as:
   - Identifying a positional prospect.
   - Going.
   - Saying something.

The names of evangelism indicate the type, setting, or target group.

- Personal Evangelism or relationship evangelism, targets those we personally know.
- Prison Evangelism targets those incarcerated.
- Servant Evangelism is helping or meeting a need first which opens a door to share the gospel.
- Teen Evangelism targets teenagers.
- Youth Evangelism targets youth in general.
- Children Evangelism targets children only.
- Evangelism Blitz is a highly concentrated effort targeting a specific community or apartment complex.
- Crusade is an open door service in a community to communicate the gospel.
- Block Party is a festive event in a community with the purpose of meeting community residents and introducing them to the church, ministry programs, and Christ.
- Medical Evangelism is providing medical services in the community with the intent of opening a door for sharing Christ.
- Web Evangelism is using the internet to share the gospel.
- Prayer Evangelism is a strategy to use prayer as a vehicle to share the gospel. Needs are prayed for first then the gospel is shared.
- International Evangelism is basically missions. It is going beyond your own borders.
- Friendship Evangelism is the same as personal evangelism.
- Door-to-Door Evangelism is going door-to-door in a community with the intent of sharing the gospel and meeting needs.
- Street Evangelism is randomly approaching people on the street.
- Event Evangelism is centered around an event.
- Track Evangelism is passing out Christian literature.
- Phone Evangelism is cold calling from a pre-generated list.
- Correspondence Evangelism is writing people to build relationships and share the gospel.

Assignment

Write a paper on one of the types of evangelism.

_____

_____

_____

_____

_____

_____

_____

_____

_____

_____

_____

_____

_____

_____

_____

_____

_____

_____

_____

_____

_____

_____

_____

_____

_____

_____

_____

_____

THE STATE OF THE UNBELIEVER

Once we know the unbeliever's state, it should motivate us to share Christ with them. Read the following Scriptures to understand the lost state of the unbeliever:

1. Under sin (Rom. 3:9)

2. Unrighteous (Rom. 3:10)

3. Guilty before God (Rom. 3:19)

4. Fallen Short of God's glory (Rom. 3:23)

5. Enemies of God (Rom. 5:10)

6. Under a death sentence (Rom. 6:23)

7. Spiritually dead to the things of God (1 Cor. 2:14–16)

8. Blinded by Satan (2 Cor. 4:3–4)

9. Possessed (Mark 5: 1–20)

10. Prisoner (2 Tim. 2:26)

11. Dead in trespasses and sins; walking according to demonic influences; fulfilling the desires of the flesh and mind; children of wrath; having uncircumcised hearts; without Christ; aliens to the commonwealth of Israel; strangers to the covenant and promises of God; hopeless; and without God in this world (Eph. 2).

The above Scriptures reveal the lost state of the unbeliever. He or she is under sin, unrighteous, guilty before God, fallen short of His glory, an enemy of God, under a death sentence, and spiritually blind. Paul in the Ephesians 2 passage, reveals a deeper state: dead in trespasses and sins (verse 1), influenced by demonic forces; fulfilling the desires of the flesh and mind (verse 2), children of God's wrath (verse 3), aliens to the commonwealth of Israel; strangers to the covenant and promises of God; hopeless; and without God in this world.

The preceding Scriptures reveal the state of those lost. Yet, God loves them so much that He sent Jesus to die for their sins and the sins of the world. When we see lost men and women, we should see them in this deprived state. This should cause us or at least remind us of our responsibility to share our faith and free them from their current state!

Witness of the Believer

God is holy, powerful, and sinless, yet He needs us to be witnesses for Him. As sinful as we are, God allows us to work with Him to win the lost. God needs a witness, and without a witness, men and women will end up in hell.

In Acts 8, God knew what the Ethiopian eunuch was reading when He sent Philip to show him the way of salvation; yet, God did not speak from heaven, He sent a man. In Acts 10, an angel spoke to Cornelius, but the divine visitor never communicated the gospel to him. God has given us the authority and responsibility to communicate the gospel to other men (Matthew 10:1–15, 28:19; Mark 16:15). Without the witness of the believer, the message will never be shared. Read the following Scriptures to understand our need to witness:

1. The commission to witness is given to men (Matthew 28:19; Mark 16:15).
2. Men testified of what they had seen and heard (1 John 1:1–3).
3. The Ethiopian eunuch asked, "How can I understand if some man does not guide me?" (Acts 8:31).
4. "Cornelius, a man will tell you what you should do" (Acts 10:1–6).
5. Paul said, "Lord, what wilt thou have me to do? And the Lord said unto him, Arise and go into the city, and it shall be told thee what thou must do" (Acts 9:6).

Notes

INTECESSORY PRAYER

P rayer is the most important ingredient in our evangelism efforts. Evangelism without prayer only results in stubborn wills and hardened hearts. Prayer is a weapon that will shatter walls of demonic resistance. We pray for three areas: the witness, the ost, and the atmosphere that surrounds them.

Things That Hinder Prayer

Before we pray, we need to confess known sin and clear the way of things that may hinder ur prayers. The following are some things that may hinder our prayer life.

- Turning ones ear from the Law (Proverbs 28: 9–13)
- Regarding iniquity in your heart (Psalm 66:18)
- Lack of faith (Mark 11: 23)
- Unforgiveness (Mark 11: 25)
- Division in relationships (1 Peter 3:7)
- Demonic forces (Daniel 10: 1–13)
- Not praying according to divine pattern (1 Timothy 2:1–6)
- Indifference (Proverbs 1:28)
- Neglect of mercy (Proverbs 21: 13)
- Stubbornness (Zechariah 7: 13)
- Instability (James 1:6–7)
- Self-indulgence (James 2:3)

Personal Prayer

The witness is encouraged to maintain a devotional life of prayer, reading and meditating n God's Word, and living out biblical principles in God's Word. We must develop our ersonal prayer life before we can effectively pray for others. We want to maintain a clean ife so we can hear God and be used by Him in order to be effective witnesses.

When we are not consistent in these areas, we tend to gravitate to our flesh and we vill lose our desire to witness. If we are clean before the Lord, we can then have confi- ence to intercede and pray for others. *Beloved, if our heart condemn us not, then have we confidence toward God* (1 John 3:21). Out of a consistent, fervent prayer life, one become committed and can then surrender his will to God's. Through prayer, we become mor sensitive to the lost and can ascertain God's heart of concern for them. Through prayer a passion for hurting and lost people will surface in our lives. The lack of compassion indicates we are not spending much time in prayer. Compassion is the heart of God. In fact, according to Matthew 9:35, God has an active compassion. The compassion He feel, causes a response.

When we are not consistent in our prayer and meditation in God's Word, we begin a decline and begin to engage in fleshly activities. Second, we lose our desire to see lost men and women come to know Jesus.

Praying for Church Members

We are all called to share our faith. Yet, in most churches where evangelism exists, only a few are obedient to the primary call of the church.

Some church members are held in bondage; fear and deception chain them to thei pews. We are all called to share our faith. The following lists ways to pray for othe church members:

- Pray against the powers of darkness, apathy, unbelief, and rebellion.
- Pray that laborers to go into the mission field (Matthew 9:37–38). Jesus said that the fields are white and ready to harvest, but the laborers are few.
- Pray that God releases a spirit of evangelism in the church. In Acts 1:8, when the Holy Spirit fell on them, He brought a spirit of evangelism to reach beyond Jerusalem.
- Pray against the powers of darkness and the spirits of apathy, unbelief and rebellion that hold us in our pews (Daniel 10:13, Ephesians 6).
- Pray that God raises up laborers to go into the mission field (Matthew 9:37,38) Jesus said that the fields were white all ready to harvest, but the laborers were few (John 4:35). Ask God to raise up church members who will answer the call to share Christ with a dying world. Jesus said that we should pray to the Lord of Harvest to raise labors to gather the harvest (Matthew 9:38). For eyes to be opened to God' calling, our inheritance and the power that is available to us, which is the same powe that raised Christ from the dead. Ephesians 1:18–20 specifically teaches us what we should pray for our fellow believers
- Pray for the lost that do not know Christ.
- Pray for the atmosphere of the community and the demolition of territorial spirits.

- Ask God to raise up church members who will answer the call to share Christ with a dying world. Jesus said we should pray to the Lord of the harvest to raise laborers to gather the harvest (Matthew 9:38).

Praying for the Lost

The lost are held in bondage by a cruel taskmaster, Satan. His only desire is to steal, kill, and destroy (John 10:10). He wants to sift men like wheat (Luke 22:31) and hold them in bondage (2 Timothy 2:26). According to Ephesians 2:3, men and women live according to the pattern of this world, fulfilling the lusts of our flesh and minds. So, we need to set people free from the clutches of Satan. We invest significant time in methods to attack the lost. Yet, praying, intercession and fasting (according to Isaiah 58) will yield extraordinary results. When God's Spirit draws the lost, then He alone receives the glory. He is the great evangelist. The first biblical example is God leading all those wild animals into the ark of safety in Genesis 6. Our prayers of intercession should be specific. The following are ways to pray for those held in bondage:

- Power of demonic spirits to be broken (Luke 4:33).
- God the Heavenly Father to draw the lost to himself (John 6:44).
- Against spiritual blindness (2 Cor. 4:3–4, Ephesians 1:18).
- The Holy Spirit to convict the lost (John 16:8). A man will never be convicted of his sin unless the Holy Spirit reveals it to him. He cannot be saved until he first feels lost!

Mark 4 describes different types of soils, which represent the heart. If the soil is hard, the heart is hard. If the soil is soft, the heart can receive the seed of God's Word. We need to pray for God to give the lost person a receptive heart.

- Repentance (2 Timothy 2:25).
- God's goodness leads people to repent (Romans 2:4).

Praying Over the Atmosphere

Most times when we pray for the lost, we only pray for them to be saved, neglecting the influence of unseen spiritual forces that hold them in bondage. We need to pray against forces of darkness that have oppressed and controlled them. In Ephesians 6:12, Paul reminds us that our struggle is against principalities, powers, rulers of darkness, and spiritual wickedness in high places.

First Peter 5:8 tells us that Satan goes through the earth as a lion, seeking to devour people. He personally attacks them and the atmosphere. In our prayers, we need to ask God to release them from demonic forces and hindering spirits. Our prayers should be directed against powers of darkness in the name of Jesus Christ! We should remind Satan that the blood of Jesus is against him! The power we have is the same as that which raised Jesus from the grave (Eph. 1:19–20).

We cannot assume the lost will automatically come to Christ. We must help them. Satan has blinded the lost (2 Cor. 4:3–4) and desires to destroy them. Through prayer and fasting, which means to abstain for a time from food or some other item desired, God begins the process of deliverance and salvation.

Prayer Walking

Prayer walking is very effective and has its biblical basis in Joshua 6, as the children of Israel lay siege to Jericho. As church members walk or drive through the neighborhood, they can pray for the residents, against demonic forces, and simply claim the neighborhood for God.

A sample prayer list is on the following page. Church members are encouraged to write the names of family members, co-workers, friends and loved ones. They can also write the names of people in their neighborhood or apartment complex. The list should then be given to the prayer ministry for intercession. Members are also encouraged to fast or abstain from food or anything that is dear to you for a period of time. Isaiah 58:5–11 tells us that God has chosen a fast "to loose the bands of wickedness, to undo the heavy burdens, and to let the oppressed go free."

Encourage churches and members to fast and pray weekly for those names on their list and for lost persons in general. Pray for the individual and over the atmosphere. Have participants fill out the list at the end of this session. Through prayer and the working of the Holy Spirit:
- The church will be on one accord.
- God will release a spirit of evangelism in the church.
- God will raise up laborers to go into the mission field.
- The eyes of the congregation will be opened to the power that is available to them through the Holy Spirit.
- Doors will be opened to witness and ministry.
- Yokes will be broken over the lives of family members, loved ones, coworkers, neighbors, and friends.
- People will repent, believe and accept Jesus as their Savior.
- Break the chains of fear, apathy and rebellion that hold church members in their pews.

- Prick the hearts of your congregation so they will have compassion for people who are hurting and lost.
- Break down walls of resistance among those to whom you will witness and replace them with receptive hearts.
- Enlist the power of the Holy Spirit to lead, direct, speak, convict and draw the lost.

Evangelism without prayer only results in a stubborn will and a hard heart in those whom we try to reach. In Joshua 3:11, the people did not move unless the Ark of the Covenant, symbolizing God's presence, went before them.

Likewise, we must have God's presence go ahead of us to assure victory. Like David, we should ask the Lord in what direction He wants us to go. David wanted God to go before him. If God was not going before him, he knew he could not prevail in battle (1 Samuel 30). Without prayer, we will find ourselves engaged in demonic activity that could have been held back through our efforts in prayer.

MY PRAYER LIST

"God forbid that I should sin against the LORD in ceasing to pray for you…"
1 Samuel 12:23

1. _____

2. _____

3. _____

4. _____

5. _____

6. _____

7. _____

8. _____

9. _____

10. _____

11. _____

12. _____

13. _____

14. _____

15. _____

Notes

_____

_____

_____

_____

_____

_____

_____

_____

_____

_____

_____

_____

_____

_____

_____

_____

_____

Make a commitment to pray for those on your prayer list and others daily. Along with prayer, set aside a day to fast for them according to Isaiah 58, to break the bands of wickedness, undo heavy burdens, and set captives free.

UNDERSTANDING DEMOGRAPHICS

If you are involved with any type of evangelism or planting a church, demographics are an important component in the process. The question may be asked, what are demographics and how can they help my efforts? Where do I find demographic information?

Demographic information refers to information describing a population within a given geographic area. Information includes such items as age, income, marital status, occupations, number and age of children, and additional information. The information can be obtained at your local library, or you can simply Google the information needed by providing the name of the city and request demographic information.

Demographic information contains information about a person's status, age and occupation, but does not give information about what a person thinks, believe, how they behave, and what is important to them. To obtain this information, one must go beyond basic demographics.

Obtaining information about a person's values, beliefs, lifestyle, and so on is more difficult. While looking for this type of information we should research additional sources such as:

Sociological Demographics

This is the study of human social behavior. Why do people do what they do? Patterns and behavior is the focus.

Psychographics

Psychographics refers to information on attitudes, values, opinions, and beliefs. This information is important in understanding how to connect with people.

Praxiographics

Praxiographics refers to information on what people do, how they behave, where they go, what they are involved in, how much they give and so on. This information is important when designing outreach ministries.

Mediagraphics

Mediagraphics refers to information on how people receive information. This is important when trying to figure out how to get information and also how to get your information heard.

The best way to obtain information in the latter three is by surveying the community and asking questions. However, I feel very strong about the way we survey. This will be discussed in the strategy section of this manual.

Demographics are simply information. Demographics can never take the place of what God desires to do within your community. Regardless of the resources we employ, the greatest results will be experienced as we seek God for His plan for our community, and then move out using resources to aid us in our efforts.

Sources of Demogrphic Information

The following are sources on where to obtain demographic information:
- Board of Realtors
- Chamber of Commerce
- Libraries
- UCC Research Office (www.census.gov)
- U.S Census Bureau (www.marketingtools.com)
- American Demographics

Assignment

Students are to compile demographics for one of the following and bring to class. The demographics should contain the following information: population based on gender, household income based on household, race, crime, unemployment, education of residents and labor. Some demographic information will include religion and political affiliation.
- A city
- A county
- A state
- A country
- A zip code

Notes

Gospel Presentation & Testimony

This session is designed to teach the student how to effectively witness to your congregation, whether large or small. At the end of the two-hour training, people who have never shared the gospel are ready to witness to others immediately. For best results, we recommend role-playing the testimony and gospel presentation portions. To break the fear associated with witnessing, we recommend immediate participation once the workshop is complete. This means intentionally witnessing the same day. The workshop can be given in its entirety, designed for two hours (depending on the facilitator), or just the testimony and gospel presentation may be taught, which can be completed in one hour.

We recommend that at a minimum, training should include the testimony portion and gospel presentation.

Before we begin, we need to discuss those things that hinder us from fulfilling the Great Commission.

- Fear
- Lack of training
- Assuming the responsibility to evangelize is that of the evangelist or pastor
- Lack of commitment
- Persecution
- Lack of compassion

While these are certainly the obvious, there are others we may not be so familiar with. In his book *A Heart for the City,* John Fuder lists the things that hinder us from moving out with compassion. He references Matthew 9:36, where the Scripture says "but when Jesus saw the multitudes, He was moved with compassion on them." He describes the compassion of God as "active," one that goes beyond a feeling, or a knowledge of the need but moves on what is being felt. He describes three things that hinder our compassion or response to others in need of receiving the gospel.

First, we are too quick to condemn others for where they are in life, rather than move with compassion and help them or share Christ. Second, we are filled with curiosity relative to how they got in the condition they are in. In John 9, the disciple asked the question, who did sin, he or his parents? Fuder says their theological curiosity was more important than the need or condition to minister. Jesus' response was that it was for the glory of God. Third, the cultural chasm that exits between races. Jesus went beyond cultural boundaries to meet the need of the Samaritan woman. As long as we refuse to cross racial, ethnic, and cultural lines, the compassion of Jesus will not be released through us to minister to their needs or lead them to Christ. If we only reach those of our own cultural persuasion, we segregate the gospel of Christ.

Compassion is cultivated by going where the need is. As long as we express our compassion from the pew, it will only be felt from the heart. When I begin to move towards others it then becomes an active compassion. Fuder says, if we don't move in the direction of those who are hurting, "our heart is far from the place the heart of God gets busy."

I have found that just as Satan blinds us to receive Christ; he blinds us to share Christ. We have all heard people say, "I wish I had given my life to Christ years ago. Once a person breaks the chains that have them chained to the pew, and purpose to approach someone to share the gospel, their eyes come open and they make the same statement about witnessing. "Why haven't I done this before?"

The Witness of the Believer

God is holy, powerful, and sinless, yet He needs us to be witnesses for Him. As sinful as we are, God allows us to work with Him to win the lost. God needs a witness, and without a witness, men and women will end up lost without Christ, doomed to an eternal hell.

In Acts 8, God knew that the Ethiopian eunuch was reading the scroll of Isaiah when He sent Philip to show him the way of salvation; yet, God did not speak from heaven, He sent a man. In Acts 10, an angel spoke to Cornelius, but the divine visitor never communicated the gospel to him. In Acts 9, Jesus himself appeared to Saul, but never told him how to be saved. Paul's conversion came days later at the home of Ananias. God has given us the authority and responsibility to communicate the gospel to other men (Matt. 10:1–15; 28:19; Mark 16:15). Without the witness of the believer, the message will never be shared. Read the following Scriptures to understand our need to witness:

- The commission to witness is given to men (Matt. 28:19; Mark 16:15).
- Men testified of what they had seen and heard (1 John 1:1–3).
- The Ethiopian eunuch asked, "How can I understand if some man does not guide me?" (Acts 8:31).
- "Cornelius, a man will tell you what you should do" (Acts 10:1–6).
- Paul said, "Lord, what wilt thou have me to do? And the Lord said unto him, Arise and go into the city, and it shall be told thee what thou must do" (Acts 9:6).

The Father did not tell the Ethiopian eunuch how to be saved. The Angel did not tell Cornelius, nor did Jesus tell Paul, yet, the Holy Spirit does reveal Jesus (John 16:14). In each case a man had to be the one that communicated the message of salvation. God has given the Great Commission to men. If we don't communicate the message of the gospel people will die and go to hell, and God will allow it!

God's Word in the New Birth

The following are just a few Scriptures that indicate the importance of God's Word in the process of the new birth. God's Word cleanses us. His Word softens the hardened heart, allowing the Word to be received. Faith comes by hearing the Word. Once the Word is received, God's power is released and a spiritual birth takes place.

- God's Word cleans (Psalm 119:9). God's Word breaks up the hardness in our hearts (Jeremiah 23:29).
- God's Word is like a sword (Ephesians 6:17).
- God's Word builds faith for salvation (Romans 10:17; John 20:31).
- God's Word is the power to save (Romams 1:16).
- We are born again by God's Word (1 Peter 1:23).

God's Word is the only solution that will cleanse our sins. Church membership does not save us or cleanse us. His Word breaks the hardness of our hearts. His Word, according to Hebrews 4:15, goes into our joints and effects change. His Word produces faith that we can change and gives us hope of eternal life. This releases the power of God that changes our heart and produces a salvation experience.

The Holy Spirit in the Life of the Lost

The Holy Spirit is at work in the life of the lost. Read the following Scriptures to see how the Holy Spirit is at work:

- He precedes the witness (Acts 9, 10). He has already worked on the heart of the lost person. We call this a "divine appointment."
- He convicts the world of sin (John 16:8). One role of the Holy Spirit is to initiate conviction. You do not have to point out sin in the unbeliever's life they know it!
- He reveals God's existence (Rom. 1:18–23). Nature reveals God exists. This is "general revelation." "Specific revelation" is a personal knowledge of Christ. The point is, nature witnesses the existence of God.

The Holy Spirit is already at work in the salvation process. He works in the life of the witness (see notes in "The Witness of the Believer" section). In the lost, He is working to reveal the need for a changed life and to bring about sorrow for sins committed against God. According to the first chapter of Romans, the Holy Spirit reveals the existence of God through nature. Men through the ages have always acknowledged a higher power. This is evident through hieroglyphic writings on walls and demonstrated by people that worship deities other than God. Through their worship, men acknowledge the existence of a higher power, but don't know his name.

As Paul did in Acts 17:23, we have to declare His name to those that don't know Him. God has placed a void or an unfulfilled place in the hearts of all lost persons. Unbelievers seek to fulfill this void or unfulfilled place through sin and pleasure. However, it will never be fulfilled until one receives Christ in their heart by faith.

The Holy Spirit in the Life of the Witness

The Holy Spirit prepares the witness by empowering him to share the gospel. He gives us words to say and places those with receptive hearts in our lives so we can share Christ with them.

- He enables the believer (Acts 1:8).
- He gives us boldness (Acts 4:30–31).
- He helps our inadequacies (Luke 12:12).
- He creates divine appointments (John 4:1–30; Acts 8:30, 9:10–16).

The Holy Spirit empowers the believer to witness, gives us boldness, gives us words to say, and creates opportunities for us to share our faith to those who do not know Christ. As we yield ourselves to the Holy Spirit, He gives us power. That means we have to move out in faith. Witnessing is as simple as identifying a lost person, moving toward them, and then saying something.

Tools in Our Hands

God has given us some tools we can use to share the Gospel. Listed below are a few:

Invitation

The woman at the well was so excited about her encounter with Jesus that she left her water pot. She ran back to the village and told the men, *Come, see a man, which told me all things that ever I did: is not this the Christ?* (John 4:29).

I believe these men knew her and they responded to her invitation. Many people will respond to the invitation based on our excitement.

Excitement

Can you imagine Andrew coming to Peter and saying, "Hey man I have found the Christ!" and Andrew replying, "Yeah, right!"? The Jews were looking for the Messiah. There may have been others who said they were the Christ. Perhaps, it was excitement that caused

Peter to go with Andrew. If we are not excited about our Lord and our church, how can we expect others to be excited?

Prayer

We can use prayer as a tool to open a door to share the gospel. In Acts 9:32–42, Peter prayed for two people. One was dead, and the other was sick. God raised one from the dead and healed the other. Prayer is one of our greatest tools. Sometimes the only thing we can do to meet a need is pray. Once we have prayed with a person for their needs, then we can share Christ. Jesus always met the natural need first. This gave Him the privilege to speak or share with the people. Prayer opened the door. We will broaden prayer in the strategy section.

Personal Testimony

Your life story is called your testimony. People may argue with you about Scriptures, but they cannot dispute a strong testimony because it is factual. Your testimony consists of three parts, modeled by Paul in Acts 26:

1. What your life was like before you received Christ.

2. Your salvation experience.

3. How your life has changed since you accepted Christ.

You should be able to share your testimony in two to three minutes. Begin with the question, "May I share with you the most exciting thing that has ever happened to me?" If the answer is yes, share your testimony. If no, move on. Your testimony should end by asking: "Has anything like this ever happened to you?" If no, ask permission to share the gospel, which we will discuss next. (Stop now, get a partner, and practice your testimony.)

My Testimony

"May I share with you the most exciting thing that has ever happend to me?"

My Life Before Christ

_____
_____
_____
_____
_____
_____
_____
_____

My Salvation Experience

_____
_____
_____
_____
_____
_____
_____
_____

Since I Accepted Christ

_____
_____
_____
_____
_____
_____
_____
_____

"Has anything like this ever happened to you?"

Leader: Instruct participants to write their personal testimony. Instruct participants to write at the top of the page: "May I share with you the most exciting thing that has ever happend to me?" At the bottom of the page, write "Has anything like this ever happened to you?"

During a conversation with anyone at anytime, the question, "May I share with you the most exciting thing that has ever happened to me," can be asked. One should end by asking, "Has anything like this ever happened to you?" This will set the stage to share the gospel.

When presenting the gospel, we should always ask permission. "May I take a few minutes to share God's plan of salvation to you?" Wait for a response. If yes, say, "God has a purpose for your life, eternal life and a better life now. However, we have sin in our lives. Therefore, we must repent, which means we need to be sorry for our sins and change our current lifestyle. We must believe and accept what God has done through Jesus Christ. God was in heaven and came and lived on this earth in the person of Jesus Christ. Jesus lived on this earth and died on the cross for your sins and mine. Mr. Prospect, according to Romans 10:8–10, if you believe in your heart and confess with your mouth that Jesus died on the cross for your sins, you will be saved."

Simply tell a love story. The unsaved person most likely does not know where any Scriptures are found. Some may have problems with this. However, even though Scripture references are not mentioned, except Romans 10, the story conveyed is Scripture. Salvation is not in the numbered verses but in the story.

Encourage the new believer to pray daily and read the Scriptures. Encourage them to share their experience with others. In fact, generate a list and continue the process.

We bridge new converts over to church by creating an excitement of meeting new family members. Do you know you have a new family and they are just waiting to meet you? I hope they truly are excited and are expecting new members.

The gospel of Luke gives us an example of the excitement we should have for someone lost in Chapter 15: the lost sheep, lost coin, and lost son. Three things were lost, three things were sought after, and rejoicing was made over all three when found. Luke says the same occurs in heaven over one sinner that repents. How much more should we rejoice in our congregations?

Gospel Presentation

When we share the gospel, the message should be inviting, giving hope and causing a response—even if it is negative. Remember, you are only called to plant a seed or sprinkle water on a seed that has already been planted. God gives the increase. Do not be discouraged if you do not see immediate results. God rewards obedience, and you have done that by planting a seed. The unbeliever's response is not toward you, but God.

When you share the gospel message, as I stated above, you tell a love story. Remember, you are communicating how Jesus changed your life and gave you a hope beyond the grave. You are not trying to sell your church. Most unbelievers are turned off by our churches. The power of Christ can deliver them, so share Jesus and His power.

The message should have five points:

1. **God's Purpose**
   a. God wants us to have a better life now (John 10:10).
   b. God also wants us to have eternal life (John 3:16), but there is a problem called sin.

2. **Our Sin Nature**
   a. Sin keeps us from what God has for us (Psalm 51:5).
   b. Adam's sin was passed on to all men (Romans 5:12).
   c. All have sinned (Romans 3:23).
   d. Sin demands judgment (Romans 6:23), so we must repent!

3. **Repentance and Faith Alone**
   a. God commands all men to repent (Acts 17:30).
   b. Repent and be converted (Acts 3:19).
   c. We are saved by grace through faith, not by works (Ephesians 2:8–9).

4. **God's Plan**
   a. God came in the flesh in the person of Jesus Christ (John 1:14).
   b. Christ suffered for our sins (1 Peter 3:18).
   c. God has laid our sin on Jesus (Isaiah 53:6).

5. Surrender and Acceptance of Christ

   a. God gives us the power to become His sons or daughters (John 1:12).

   b. You must believe in your heart and confess with your mouth that Jesus is Lord of your life (Romans 10:9–10).

   c. Ask if they understand everything you say. If not, clarify!

   d. Ask them if they are ready to pray.

   e. You cannot save them, but you can lead them in a prayer, and if they mean the prayer from their heart, they will be saved.

   f. The prayer should consist of three elements:

   (1) Acknowledgement of sin—do not try to list all sin, just be truly sorry for all sins committed.

   (2) Asking God to forgive you of all your sin.

   (3) Acceptance of Christ

Notes

I purpose to share my testimony and the gospel to the following lost family members, friends, coworkers and neighbors. List their names:

_____

_____

_____

_____

_____

_____

_____

_____

_____

_____

_____

_____

_____

_____

_____

_____

_____

_____

_____

_____

_____

_____

_____

_____

Recommendations

The follow-up process is a very important component in evangelism work. Without the committed efforts of those who follow up, our churches are mere revolving doors. Although our focus in this manual is on those we evangelize, we should broaden our follow-up to include inactive members of our churches and visitors. In addition, I suggest preparing a manual that lists contact information, available services and guidelines for referring people to:

• Ministries within your church
• Ministries in other churches and para-church ministries in your local area
• Government agencies in the area

Sometimes we do not have resources on hand to meet the needs of those we minister. A referral list will solve this problem. The most important thing is to meet their needs. Wouldn't it edify the church and give glory to God if the person's became a messenger of the church by saying, "that church met my needs or sent me to blank place, rather than saying, they take in all that money or the preacher drives or lives a certain way but they cannot help people.

The following information is critical for successful follow up:

1. Name, address, and phone numbers

2. Prospect's response (received Christ, rededication, assurance of salvation)

3. Prayer needs

4. Follow-up needs (need for food, shelter, or help with utilities, job-related, or visitation requested)

A Few More Things to Consider

If we are working within the community, it's important how we represent the kingdom as well as not to stand in the way of sinners (Psalms 1). In other words, we do not hinder people from receiving Christ.

• Dress appropriately for the community and not church.
• Knocking on the door, tell them the church has been praying for them. You have come by to personally share our concern for their family and personally pray for them. Ask, "Do you have any needs we may pray for at this time?" After prayer an invitation for Christ or a personal invitation to attend church should be given.
• Make a personal phone call within 24 hours after a witnessing experience.

- The witness should be the primary person to follow up.
- Follow-up means also following up on personal needs.
- If the person does not desire to attend your church, help him or her find one, or at least suggest one.
- Follow-up means mentoring. Make sure they get plugged into church, Bible study and other church functions. Remember, we are not just after a convert. We have not fulfilled the Great Commission until we make a disciple.
- Make sure they have transportation. There could be a member who lives close by or within the same zip code that will be willing to help. If we are not willing to follow-up, we should not evangelize. It would be like having a baby and abandoning it!

Discipleship

Discipleship is very important and must be a part of the evangelism process. The activity of the commission is going, baptizing, and teaching. Christ's command to make disciples provides our scriptural mandate. Teach what Jesus taught. Disciples follow Jesus.

As I stated earlier, we can produce many converts when we share the gospel. However, we have not fulfilled the Great Commission if we have not made another disciple! Discipleship is a component of three parts:

1. We evangelize with the intent of sharing the gospel with someone lost.

2. We assist with their spiritual growth.

3. They mature and enter into ministry to others. We are not only responsible for leading someone to Christ, but also for caring for him and his spiritual development after the salvation experience.

This can be done by using some of the following suggestions:

- The person who led them to Christ should be the primary person responsible. Mentor them. Follow up on their participation in church, new member's class, Sunday school, and Bible study. Make sure they get to church. If they need a ride, pick them up.
- Make yourself available if they need to call you and ask questions.
- Pray for them. Paul continued to pray for the converts until Christ was formed in them (Galatians 4:19). He prayed until he knew Christ had gotten hold of their heart. This means they come to church without being asked.

- Encourage them. The Christian life is foreign to them. They are not use to our Christian lifestyle or vernacular. It is not easy for them to live the principles in God's Word, so encourage them and be there for them.
- Make another soul-winner, and teach them what you know.

Just like salesmen, encourage them to make a list of those they want to receive Christ, and visit with them. Remember, they are excited, so keep them that way. If they see us sitting and not witnessing, they will do the same; how we live relative to our faith and practice become critical as we disciple others.

Reflection Questions

1. How important is discipleship?

_____

_____

_____

_____

_____

_____

2. Does your church disciple new converts?

_____

_____

_____

_____

_____

3. How active are you in the discipleship process of those you win to Christ?

_____

_____

_____

_____

_____

_____

Report Form

Ministry_____ Date _____

❏ Prayer Workshop   ❏ Evangelism Workshop   ❏ Blitz   ❏ Personal Visit

Action   ## Quantity

Shared Christ   _____

Received Christ   _____

Assured of Salvation   _____

Rededication   _____

Prayed for Needs   _____

Enrolled in Sunday School   _____

Total Contacts   _____

First-Time Participants   _____

Total Participants   _____

Monthly Personal Visits   _____

Monthly Blitz   _____

Monthly Prayer Training   _____

Monthly Evangelism Training   _____

Before engaging in ministry to others, we suggest the following prayer:

"Heavenly Father, bless our efforts as we represent you in the earth. May your presence and power go before us and with us. Give us words to say that will penetrate the hearts of those we encounter today. Open our ears so we may hear what you are saying to us. Most of all, let our efforts expand your kingdom and bring glory to your name. In Jesus' name, amen."

Notes

EVANGELISM STRATEGIES

Within this chapter I will introduce several effective strategies for successful evangelism. Before I do, I believe it is very important we establish that God is the great evangelist, who by the Holy Spirit draws lost people. Second, it is also important that we establish the importance of prayer in our efforts. We have discussed prayer in chapter 3. Without prayer, the impoverished life of the witness will be revealed and we will encounter demonic residence.

Joshua Ministry Strategy

The Joshua Ministry is based on a strategy that mobilizes the body of Christ to go into their communities and help their lost brothers and sisters "possess" their land, take back what Satan has stolen from them. This strategy may be used by any church of any denomination to kindle a passion for unsaved people in their congregations and to systematically share the gospel and disciple the lost within our member's communities.

The Joshua Ministry is based on biblical principles from the Book of Joshua. As the Israelites where preparing to enter the Promised Land, Joshua called together the tribes of Reuben, Gad and Manasseh and reminded them of the commission Moses had given to "help your brothers possess their land." "And to the Reubenites, the Gadites and the half-tribe of Manasseh, Joshua said, remember the command that Moses the servant of the LORD gave you: The LORD your God is giving you rest and has granted you this land. Your wives, your children and your livestock may stay in the land that Moses gave you east of the Jordan, but all your fighting men, fully armed, must cross over ahead of your brothers. You are to help your brothers until the LORD gives them rest, *as he has done for you*, and until they too have taken possession of the land that the LORD your God is giving them. After that, you may go back and occupy your own land, which Moses the servant of the LORD gave you east of the Jordan toward the sunrise" (Joshua 1:12–15).

Just as Joshua reminded the Israelites to cross the Jordan to help their brothers possess their land, we, too, must cross over any obstacle to help our brothers and sisters evangelize their neighborhoods and meet the needs of others until their communities are possessed by God.

I heard on a talk show recently in which the subject was evangelism in our post modern world. The conscience from those that called in as well as the talk show host was that the church needs to discard conventional forms of evangelism and exclusively use the internet. While I believe internet evangelism is one form of evangelism and that we use technology to evangelize, we should use any means to win others. On the other hand I think it is important that we don't allow technology take the place of touching and ministering to people. There are some that would argue the point relative to what He meant when He said "go." There is no substitute for personal ministry. Nor should we seek to replace it!

Unity Strategy

The following strategy is from my book, *Unity, the Highest Form of Evangelism:*

I am convinced "unity" is the highest form of evangelism. As we move forward, I am going to spend more time on this strategy than others. I feel very strong about unity in the body of Christ and about those things that hinder unity.

We probably all can agree that much can be achieved when people work together in unity for the same cause. When I think of people working together for one cause, two select passages of Scripture come to mind.

The first is found in Genesis chapter 11, the Tower of Babel. The second is found in Nehemiah 4:6: "and the people had a mind to work." Both passages demonstrate what can be achieved when people intentionally come together, in unity, with the same purpose and a mind to work. These Scriptures indicate their willingness to work together, and their ability to achieve the task. Actually, if God had not intervened in the Genesis passage, they would have achieved their task and built a tower that reached heaven. What was it about their efforts that aroused God and got His attention? I believe it was the oneness they displayed. There was no division in their purpose or effort. The Scripture says "behold, the people are one" (Genesis 11:6). I would like to believe this oneness, or unity, caught God's attention, and resulted in a personal visitation from him. Before this visitation from heaven, the only other visitation from God to man was with Adam (Genesis 1–2). God had appeared to Adam in the cool of the evening and had fellowship with him. However, there is no suggestion of fellowship or relationship between God and those in the Genesis 11 account. Yet, the mere fact that they worked together and would have achieved their task, got God's attention, and he responded from heaven. I would like to strongly suggest that before this time, God had paid little attention to those in the Genesis 11 text. I would like to suppose the unity they displayed got His attention because it displayed the same unity that was displayed in heaven between the Godhead, and the unity He expressly desired to be proven to a dying world before the return of Christ. I believe unity is what God desires for His body and is the highest form of evangelism.

As I stated in the introduction, the five-fold ministry gifts: apostles, prophets, evangelist, pastors and teachers, according to Ephesians 4:11–13, are to equip or teach the "body" until she walks and lives in unity. The five-fold ministry gifts are to teach us, until we all come into the unity of faith, and into the knowledge of the Son of God, unto a mature man. The unity or oneness Paul spoke about would bring us to a place that we are persuaded and rely upon Christ for salvation. Unity would mean that we are fully mature. Aside from this, I do not know what that entails. Will it mean we agree on all points of doctrine, procedure, or policy? Probably not; however, it does mean we are to unify in what the Ephesians passage calls, "the unity of the faith."

The "unity of the faith" could mean different things to different believers, however, I would like to suggest for your consideration, what I believe the "unity of the faith" could be. I believe the "unity of the faith" is not the name of any denomination, church, or para-church ministry. Rather, the "unity of the faith" is the common "faith," we share in Jesus, and what He provided through his sacrificial death at Calvary. The death and resurrection of Jesus are the exclusive occurrence that unites us as one. The resurrection unites all orthodox churches, catholic churches, and protestant churches. The cross is the single event that should unite us and our work in God's kingdom. The unity that we display should have such an affect that it draws the unbeliever beneath the Savior's cross. The result of our prayer is directly related to the prayer Jesus prayed before his death, and what He expected to occur.

In John 17, Jesus' prayed an interesting prayer. What is the significance of this prayer? More than anything, this was His request before His death. The prayer was for unity. How can we effectively fulfill the Great Commission if we are not one with each other and with Jesus and the Father?

The first request Jesus made was that He be glorified. He expressly desired to be restored with the glory He laid aside when He robed himself in humanity. According to Philippians 2:6–7, He laid aside His divinity and came in the likeness as man. Second, He prayed that the disciples be sanctified or set apart for the use of God. Jesus prayed that God would keep them from the world. They were to be in the world but not part of the world. He wanted them to be kept from the evil of the world (John 17:6–19). Thirdly, He prayed for those who would, down through history, believe on the message of the gospel. His prayer was that those who believed, received the message and became His disciples would come to a place of unity. This unity would have such an impact on the world that the lost would know that God had sent him. The direct result would be that the world would know without a doubt that He was sent by God! The effect would be that unity between the members of His body, would witness to the world that Christ is the answer. The church has yet manifested such unity. This unity is displayed between Jesus and the Father, and based on His prayer, should be in us. The world should see in us, in visible form, the unity that exists between Jesus and the Father. This unity should bring us together in thought, purpose, and action relative to the Great Commission. I believe the church; the body of Christ, at this point is fragmented and this form of unity alludes us. If this statement is true, that we are fragmented and if fragmented, we are in need of healing. How then can we bring healing to others if we need healing ourselves? The church will fulfill God's intent; Jesus guaranteed it! Jesus said "the gates of Hell will not prevail against it" (Matthew 16:18). This Scripture assures the success of the church and its unity.

Paul wrote about unity in 1 Corinthians 12, and Ephesians 4. In his letter to the church at Corinth, Paul addresses those things which hinder us from operating in unity. In the twelfth chapter, he describes how a fractional body should operate when all components are in their proper place, doing what they were made to do. It seems that Paul understood unity, and its effect relative to its function. When members of the body function apart from each other, the body can never function as it was designed, nor produce the results it should. Paul gives an example of that in 1 Corinthians 12 where the placement is given, which should produce maximum results.

The prayer of Jesus found in John 17, reflects Jesus' heartfelt desire to see his church demonstrate and exemplify what He, the Holy Spirit, and the Father epitomize daily in heaven, unity. The unity Christ prayed for is of the highest importance, for without unity our witness is hindered. In the book of Acts, the church seems to understand and live out His desired prayer for unity.

Without hesitation, I believe the church in the book of Acts lived out Jesus' prayer, and the results were compelling. What made the early Church so successful in reaching the lost? Some suggest obedience; I agree, to some extent. Yet, beyond their obedience I point to their unity. The question I raise is: Would the same results have occurred if all 120 disciples had gone back to Jerusalem and gone into their separate homes? Jesus' command was that they go back to Jerusalem and wait. He never told them to wait together at the same location, in unity. He did pray that they come together in unity (John 17:11). Perhaps this was a fulfillment of his prayer in John 17. I believe the greater results of Pentecost were not their obedience alone, but their unity. They could have been obedient, but still not together in one place, all seeking the same results. No doubt, every Christian, every church and denomination would probably say, or at least think they are obedient to God and his purpose for their church. Yet, the "body" is not unified. The question I raise is: Are our results equivalent to those of the Acts church? I am not saying we as a "body" are not doing great things, but are we doing supernatural things? Are we manifesting the same results as the Acts church did as an infant? Three thousand souls were added at one time, 5,000 on another occasion shortly thereafter (Acts 3 and 4). Some may argue, the church is producing the same results. To defend this, some would point to the fact that thousands of decisions that are made for Christ at crusade services during modern times, especially in third world countries. I agree. However, results of this proportion, as much as I can ascertain, have not been produced by the post-modern day church, but by individuals or single ministries.

I do not believe it is God's intent for the world to be won to Christ by one person, one church, one ministry, or Para-church ministry, or by on organization or denomination, but by His body coming together in unity as one.

There were four results which were byproducts of what occurred in Acts chapter two. These results for the most affected non-believers. First, fear came upon every soul (Acts 2:43). Second, wonders and signs were done by the apostles (vs. 43). Thirdly, God gave the believers favor (vs. 47). Lastly, God added to the church daily such as should be saved (vs. 47). Unity preceded these results.

There are repeated places in Acts Chapters one and two where unity is displayed. It is interesting that the words "all" and "they" appear several times in the first two chapters. In fact, "all" appears twenty-one times and the word "they" appears twenty-two times. Let's examine the times unity was displayed. Surely with so many references to unity, we must consider its importance and without fail consider that God couched it within these two chapters for a reason. This is the birth of the church! This is the infant, the baby, and she produced extraordinary results as we read within this book. If this was the baby, what will the adult look like and what will she produce? As an infant, the church proclaimed the gospel, cast out devils, healed the sick, shared, prayed together, stood together against critics, conducted business, and worshiped together, all in unity.

I believe as we demonstrate a whole body before the world, it will communicate the gospel without us saying one word. The world will know by our unity that God sent Jesus and He is the one and only way of salvation (John 17: 21–23). The results will be the same as it was in Acts 2: 43–47, with the greatest result being the addition of souls that will enter the Kingdom of God.

I believe the Acts church knew this and acted it out daily. Somewhere we have gotten away from unity. As the church progressed through the ages, especially when denominations came about, the body has become more divided.

I believe denominationalism, or mode of thinking, has inhibited the unity that was lived out among the early church and from that which God intended for us to display. I am not saying denominations are inherently evil. Denominations have done, are doing, and will continue to do ministry, deploy missionaries, and be a safe-haven for many. Yet, they have also hindered our working together and our witness to the world. Although we have diversity within our denominations we should do all we can not to allow it to bring division between us, especially as it relates to the Great Commission. Yet, the things that divide us have taken our focus off the main thing, the Great Commission. I am not saying they are not significant; however, in the light of someone being saved, a life changed, a person being transformed from the kingdom of darkness to the kingdom of God, these differences are less significant.

Hindrances Within the Body

At times our denominational mode of thinking causes more divisions and have caused paramount problems within Christendom. How can we attribute this mode of thinking as something from God when it has divided us so? The Bible clearly teaches that God is not the author of confusion. Yet, this mind-set has left the sinner confused as to what form of religion is correct, and has kept us from the main thing, the Great Commission. The lost I come in contact with, before sharing the gospel with them, converse about denominations, not Christ. Why so many denominations and so many different beliefs from one denomination and church to another?

Churches and their members talk about other churches and ministries with no regard to weak Christians or unbelievers who may be listening. I have heard professors, preachers and seminar speakers talk about other preachers and ministers, as though they were the enemy. I am not saying that I am not without guilt. However, we are family and should pray for our brothers and sisters. We seem to demonize others who are not of the devil, but born of God. The mere fact their doctrine is more liberal or conservative than what you or I believe, does not mean they are of the devil. In fact, if they believe exclusively that Jesus died and rose from the grave for their sins and they have accepted him, they are our brothers and sisters in Christ (Rom. 3:23–25). It is because of His blood we are one. If there is some misinterpreted Scripture, we should be willing to come alongside our brothers and sisters and expound to them the more excellent way, not disown them as a brother or sister. I believe this common belief in Christ is the key to the unity of the faith and should propel us to work together as Christian brothers and sisters, yet, our corporate witness will be hindered as long as we remain fragmented.

There are both obvious and subtle things that prevent unity in the body of Christ. No doubt race plays a big factor, and race is not limited to one ethnic group alone. The lines of race and the spirit of prejudice is among all peoples and groups to some degree. Great strides have been made to overcome racial barriers, yet the struggle continues both outward and inward. The most obvious struggle is demonstrated during our Sunday morning services, which suggest segregation within our congregations is a part of the gospel; at least this is what some may ascertain by our display of division. Are we communicating a separate God for each ethnic group? When we witness only to those who look like we do, we segregate the gospel. The command of Jesus to go to Jerusalem, Judea, and Samaria (Acts 1:8), and to the highways and hedges (Luke14:23), to share the gospel, suggest we go to all ethnic groups, not just our own. If we only concern ourselves with those of our own persuasion, our witness is only a Jerusalem witness. The world is not going to be won by one church or one denomination, but by one body who may have different names, but unify around Christ, His message, and the Great Commission, and won't allow doctrinal differences to separate us. These differences communicate a message of division and disunity. God is not divided nor confused; therefore, if the results are confusing, can we truly say this is of God?

Paul seemed to understand unity and how the body should react as different gifts function in one body. Paul spoke of a body of gifts not denominations. Each part of the body was a gift, placed in the body as God desired. What would be the reaction of the world if they saw, not a display of denominationalism, but a display of different gifts all functioning for the good of the body – functions to fulfill the Great Commission. The diagram on the following page illustrates our gifts working together:

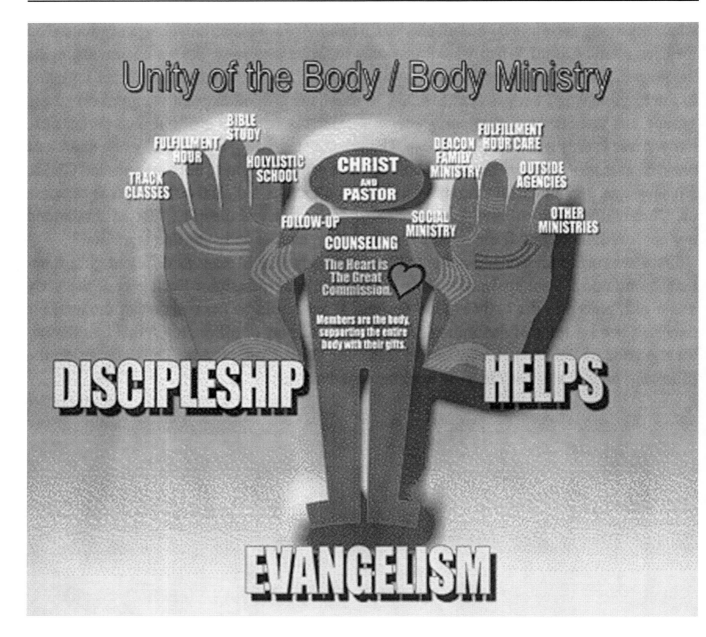

1. The head represents Christ.
2. The neck represents counseling.
3. One hand represents discipleship.
4. The other hand represents ministry.
5. The heart represents the Great Commission
6. The knees represent prayer.
7. The feet represent evangelism.

The body should represent members who function in their gifts, and support the entire body. These gifts could also be replaced by denominations that bring to the table their giftedness, or their area of specialization, all making up a complete functioning body, a ministering body to a dying world, the body of Christ.

Another area is our acceptance of church members, which is sometimes based on social, economical, political, and educational status, the haves and have-not's. These all keep the body fragmented and hinder unity. Just think of how much could be accomplished if we worked together. When natural disasters occur we work with groups of all races, vocations, social, economical, and financial statuses. Could it be that catastrophic events unify us but kingdom work does not? These hindrances directly affect our witness, our working together, and the harvest that awaits us. When we conquer these hindrances, the dying world will witness a living savior.

I see "unity" as the highest form of evangelism. Perhaps the question raised is: Why did Jesus give us the Great Commission if unity would produce a greater harvest of souls, and reveal a higher form of evangelism? Valid question; I can only say, maybe, I am not saying this is truth, but maybe God knew the body of Christ would be divided, hindering the harvest. Rather than wait for the body to come into unity, He established the Great Commission until the body unified.

Unity is a great force seen in Scripture, examples of good and evil both exist as stated earlier. Unity produced great results as people worked together. Although I propose "unity" is the highest form of evangelism, I am not discounting our current efforts, nor am I suggesting we discontinue our current efforts to reach those held by the bondage of sin. However, I am suggesting we unify so we may witness the greatest harvest of souls ever known. The current disunity within the body of Christ indicates a working power among us, but not from God.

Jesus prayed for unity in John 17, and I believe he will get His prayer answered. I hope that God does not have to use something catastrophic to bring us into a place of unity.

Before offering solutions there is one other hindrance worth discussing. This hindrance is not within the body, or what hinders the church, but some things which hinder the harvest from being reaped. There are things that the church, or that the Christian does, that hinders the harvest from being reaped. One of the greatest hindrances to receiving the harvest is hypocrisy. As we encounter numerous people who are lost, we hear story after story about how church people live among the lost. In most cases we live no different than the lost do. Jesus called one that lived in this manner a hypocrite!

In the book of St. Luke (6:39–42) Jesus said, "Can the blind lead the blind?" He is teaching them that they cannot catch a lost person if they are living the same way they live. He calls this type of lifestyle hypocrisy.

Another prejudice or hindrance is how the saint treats the sinner. Just as saints discriminate against other saints based on education, social, economical, political and others, we do the same to sinners. On Father's Day in Atlanta, a prostitute was walking down the street and heard music coming from a church. Through the music the Spirit of God begins to draw her and she decided to enter the sanctuary and participate in worship. As she entered the vestibule, an usher denied her entrance because she was a prostitute. The good thing about the story is that she went up the street and found a store front church that accepted prostitutes, drunks, those on drugs, and every other type of lifestyle some churches refuse to accept.

On another occasion I received a call from a church that had an evangelism problem and needed advice. The problem was, and I quote, "We have large numbers of teens that live next door to the church in an apartment complex and they are coming over to our church, and we do not want them at our church."

A pastor from another city called me and told me he desired to hold an outdoor service to reach the lost in his community. As he planned the service, he sent a letter to a church in the neighborhood that he was going to hold the service, since there was no place to hold the service where his church was located. He invited the church to participate, but he received no response. After holding the service he was so excited about the results but received a phone call that almost caused him to leave the ministry. On the other end of the line was an area supervisor from his denomination. You would have thought that he would have shared in his excitement; however, that was not the case. Rather, he was told that the pastor from the church he had sent the letter to wants to know why he was in his neighborhood, and that he needed to stay on his side of town. Another church began to transport teens from the inner city to their worship service. Some of the church members accepted and embraced them while others were cruel and made comments about their dress and body odor. On one occasion, one of the members cursed at two boys and told them to pull their paints up. The boys said they would never return to the church. A few months later, I inquired about the two boys and found out that one of them had been shot in the head and killed. I could not help but think that maybe the church had some responsibility in his death. Perhaps he would have taken a different direction or been at church, I cannot say.

Robert Lewis, in his book, *Church of Irresistible Influence*, says the church has burned down bridges to the community she was called to reach. I say it another way. Have you ever had a neighbor that fails to keep their property up? They are the unwanted neighbor in the neighborhood. The church has become the unwanted neighbor in the neighborhood. The status of yester years that the church had is no longer recognized. The church used to be the safe haven in the neighborhood. The church and preacher were respected. The church was the voice not only in the community, even presidents and kings looked to the church for direction. The current status of the church is one of disdain, the unwanted neighbor in the neighborhood.

I have personally witnessed churches and their treatment to homeless person who come by for help. I have witnessed members treating the lost different based on their appearance or condition of life. I have witnessed church members who did not want to take the time to help a new member based on their appearance. I have heard from those whose churches turned them off to the point they have no desire to visit again. I have witnessed the apathy towards those who live in urban communities. We act as if certain parts of our cities are Hell itself. One street person told me that the church was a pimp and the neighborhood a prostitute because the church never comes to the community until she wants something. He called it rape! By these examples, some churches decide who is acceptable to them or not. When we should be celebrating the lost receiving Christ, most members look at them as if they were a disease. This behavior is not something new; Jesus experienced the same.

The book of Luke reveals the same examples. Example: the Scribes and Pharisees are church members, the publicans are Jews who collected taxes for the Romans, and the sinners are Jews who did not keep the Law. On one occasion (Luke 5:27–32), Jesus sees a publican named Levi, who He invites to follow him. Levi is so excited that he prepares a feast and a great company of publicans and others come over. If you allow me to use my imagination, this was Jesus the pastor and Levi becomes his convert. Levi is so excited that he invites other unsaved friends to come over for food and fun. You would think the members of the church would have been excited. You would think they would have talked about God's kingdom, and minister to their needs. Their response is found in verse 30: "Why do you eat with publicans and sinners?" The members had their own exclusive club and sinners were not welcome. It's about sinners coming to Christ, fulfilling the Great Commission.

Another example is a Pharisee (church member) who desired that Jesus (pastor) would come over to his house and eat. A woman who was a "sinner" one who did not keep the Law, brought an alabaster box and began to wipe His feet with her hair (Luke 7:36–39). You would have thought the church member would have been happy that Jesus would have had an opportunity to minister to her. Yet, his response was, "If he was a prophet (pastor for our illustration) he would have known what kind of women this is, because she is a sinner!" These accounts demonstrate driving away or killing the harvest which some churches do.

People will not hear us, or our message, if we do not make them feel comfortable. Some of our churches need to learn how to receive the harvest. Why should God give us a harvest if we are going to drive it off or kill it? We need to love everyone, accept them where they are, value them as God's creation, and understand they have worth. They have potential – God has made them for a purpose and we must help them discover it. In the story of the demoniac, (Mark 5), Jesus recognized something that neither the town people nor His disciples recognized. This man had worth; He looked at him through the eyes of faith. He did not see his current state, but what he could become. There is something we miss in this text. The demoniac was not just cutting himself, but was also crying. Jesus saw that even though a demonic spirit was trying to kill him, he was crying out for help! On one hand a spirit of death and suicide was trying to end his hope of a changed life. On the other hand, he desired help! He had the same potential of any of his disciples. Jesus not only saw him trying to kill himself, but saw him calling out for a change, something no one else saw. What do we see when we look at the lost? Do we see pants hanging down, a drug addict, and a prostitute? Do we prejudge the sinner based on their appearance or lifestyle? We must look beyond what we see and accept all and not act like gate keepers. "It would be better that we have a stone around our neck and be cast into a sea than if we offend one of these little ones" (Luke 17:2).

I want to suggest some things that would promote unity among the body.

Pray for Unity

I think that if Jesus can pray for unity, we should too. We need to add this request in our daily and corporate prayer times. Along with praying for the lost, I do not see any prayer more important.

Teach Unity

We need to follow Paul's example and teach unity. It is important that we teach members the purpose of the five-fold ministry gifts that are in the "body." Along with teaching (Eph. 4) we should teach the importance of the gifts and how they function and comprise one body, the body of Christ. According to the Ephesians passage, we are to teach members of the body until unity occurs. I believe it is important that we begin to communicate the message of unity to our congregations.

Intentionally Work Together for Kingdom Building,

We must begin to purpose to work together. We are to build God's kingdom, not our own. In our quest to work for "the praise of His glory," we must first seek to embrace our differing gifts and expertise. These are not merely for our own gratification, but must be employed for the sake of the Great Commission. In other words, whatever various gifts or insights we have within the body are to be used toward fulfilling the Great Commission. Could it be that the differing gifts and grace given to all of our churches and traditions are all needed to fulfill the Great Commission? Could it be that our fragmentation prevents a greater display of his glory from being shown to the world?

There exists far too much bickering about the legitimacy of our gifts and areas of knowledge. I propose that our differences should not be debated. Rather, if any church or tradition feels that they have gifts, they should be brought to the table in fulfilling the Great Commission. If another tradition feels that they have been entrusted with guarding sound doctrine, this should be brought to the table to help keep us focused on fulfilling the mandate of our Lord. If another tradition feels that they have a greater understanding of the parish and how to care for their community, this knowledge should be shared in helping to fulfill the Great Commission.

Our differences held in debate and segregated do nothing in fulfilling the Great Commission. It is only when we bring our various flowers together for cross pollination that we see new life birthed. On the other hand, those things that in truth hold no legitimacy in God's kingdom and cannot be substantiated by Scripture will undoubtedly fall away in complete impotence as we engage the world. There will be no need for one tradition to critique another when we bring what we have to the table. Whatever is of no consequence will simply be exposed for what it is as we move out unified in the Lord's work.

This requires humility and openness. It could very well be that certain practices we find theologically discomforting are in fact of great use in fulfilling the Great Commission. On the other hand, there may be certain things we hold dear that are exposed as completely ineffective and illegitimate as we move together in fulfilling the Lord's work. The greater point here is that we need not argue over what we have or what we practice. What is needed is to bring all these things to the table together in fulfilling the Great Commission. When we do this, we will be surprised to find that certain areas of lack we have in our churches can be filled by our brothers and sisters from other traditions. When we do this, we will also find ourselves corrected by each other. Whether we experience correction or enhancement, we will find ourselves better and actively involved as one in the service of our Lord. As I write this, I am reminded of Paul's words to Timothy as it regards the Scriptures in 2 Timothy 3:16–17. Paul said, "All Scripture is given by inspiration of God, and is profitable for doctrine, for reproof, for correction, for instruction in righteousness: That the man of God may be perfect, thoroughly furnished unto all good works." In the same way, we the body, are given to each other for purposes of doctrine, reproof, correction and instruction so that we might move toward perfection. This will only happen, however, as we come together and bring what talents, gifts, expertise, and experience to the table in seeking to fulfill the Great Commission.

We have to get to the place that the only praise and glory go to God and not ourselves. This appears to be the problem at the Tower of Babel and our problem today. Everyone can not be in charge. We are all on the same team, playing for the same coach, building the same kingdom, against one foe. We must examine the reason we don't work together and begin to work past those things that hinder us. The world waits for the manifestation of the sons of God (Rom. 8:19), but we continue to demonstrate a fragmented body and hinder the harvest.

One Great Day of World Evangelism

Recently we had our first ever "One Great Day of Connection," which is properly known as "One Great Day of World Evangelism." The vision is that of Minister Jeanette Cody, a member of Greenforest Community Baptist Church where I am a member. The Lord has given her a strategy that the Body of Christ unites together on the day before Easter and shared the gospel with a lost person or invites a lost or un-churched person to church. Churches can elect to have a block-party, evangelize door-to-door, or anything they chose as long as the objective is to win the lost. Churches and individuals can register to be part of this great event at JeanetteTCody@aol.com or www.joshuaministry.com.

This one event could then be followed by a seven-month effort of seedtime and harvest. In other words, the church would go on the offense and continue to reach out and evangelize and minister to the lost and un-churched with great intensity for a period of seven months. I do not know what occurs after the seven months.

Some would be so excited about witnessing that they would continue. Perhaps Jesus would come back after our efforts—something to think about.

One-Year Strategy

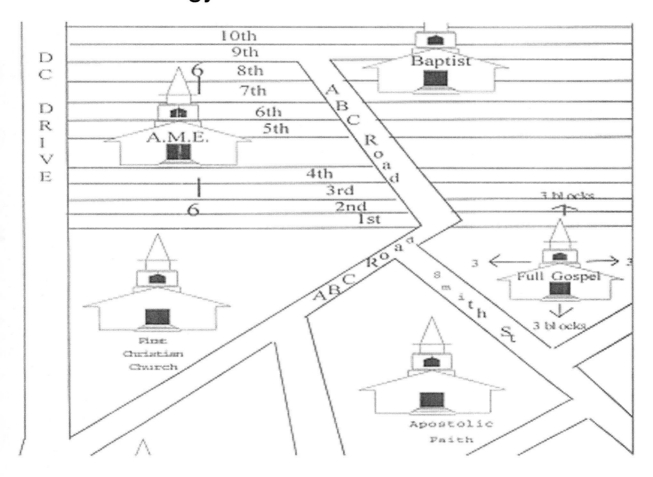

Each city, regardless of size, can be evangelized in one year. If each church, having the common ground of salvation exclusively through faith in the blood of Jesus Christ, would come together, divide the target neighborhoods into blocks, and go street-by-street, door-by-door, block-by-block, sharing the gospel and meeting needs until the next assigned area is reached. Each city could be evangelized in one year. This strategy will only work as we come together as one unit helping others possess their land. This means that although we possess different labels, we unify under the Lordship of Jesus, salvation exclusively through him, and the Great Commission. Regardless of our differences, the following, in my opinion, are the three most essential places of commonality. Each church would be responsible for a twelve-block area in which they would share Christ, disciple, and meet needs through their resources, not exclusively money, but Para-church ministries, other churches, and government agencies. Churches within the same zip code, because of the common interest they share in the community and residence, could maximize their efforts by working together in unity. We are only sharing Christ and not doctrinal views. Churches could join in a selected community and represent a host church, repeating the same process in other areas, helping each other possess their land. Read more about this strategy in my book, *The Joshua Ministry*, (based on the principle of helping your brother possess his land). Joshua told the members of the tribes of Reuben, Gad, and Manasseh to cross over the Jordan River and help their brothers possess their land. The tribes of Reuben, Gad, and Manasseh desired their inheritance on the other side of the river where they were only allowed their inheritance if they crossed over and helped their brothers possess their land (Josh 1:13, 14). Moses understood that a joint effort would yield the greatest results. You can read more about this strategy in the Joshua series books at www.joshuaministry.com.

House Church/Incarnation Strategy

When I was on staff as minister of evangelism, I drew a circle representing I-285, the interstate which goes around the city of Atlanta. Through that circle I drew lines which represent I-75, I-85, and I-20. Both I-75 and I-85 go north and south, I-20 east and west. I took a marker and indicated in green the location of our church, and a different color marker identified places where we had existing home Bible studies. The principle was demonstrated by Jesus as He left his divinity and took upon Himself the likeness of mere men. It means becoming part of that community. The church would be involved in every aspect of the community. The ministry of the church would become holistic in nature ministering to the whole man, spirit, (the spiritual man), soul (the mind or education), and body (the physical part). We could work together by planting a house church in a home or apartment complex. As the resident lives in the community and develops relationships, ministers to needs, is involved in all aspects of the community as a resident in the community, he or she will be fulfilling the following passage from Isaiah 32:2–3. "As we become a hiding place from the wind for the residence; and as we become a cover from the tempest, and a shadow in a weary land. Then their eyes will be open and they will hear us." As we develop the people we would solicit the help from trained associates who are waiting for an opportunity to minister. Ministers could come from churches of different denominations but have as a point of unity, salvation in Christ. This process would then be duplicated in another area, and then another until the entire city was affected. I do not know how long this would take. Some may feel this is too simplistic, yet God has chosen the simple things.

Set the Captives Free! Strategy

Set the Captives Free strategy is designed to engage the entire congregation to fulfill the Great Commission. As members generate a list of unsaved family members, friends, loved-ones, neighbors, and co-workers; continued prayer and fasting are a must by members that participate. The following Scripture is a biblical basis for helping members possess their land:

"But to the Reubenites, the Gadites and the half-tribe of Manasseh, Joshua said, remember the command that Moses the servant of the Lord gave you: The Lord your God is giving you rest and has granted you this land.' Your wives, your children and your livestock may stay in the land that Moses gave you east of the Jordan, but all your fighting men, fully armed, must cross over ahead of your brothers. You are to help your brothers until the Lord gives them rest, as he has done for you, and until they too have taken possession of the land that the Lord your God is giving them. After that, you may go back and occupy your own land, which Moses the servant of the Lord gave you east of the Jordan toward the sunrise" (Joshua 1:12–15 NIV).

Church members help others "possess their land" or evangelize their neighborhoods. Members can also accompany other members during personal visits and mentor them.

Through the power of the Spirit of God, church members free family members, friends, neighbors, and coworkers with prayer and intentional witnessing.

"The Spirit of the Lord is upon me, because he hath anointed me to preach the gospel to the poor; he hath sent me to heal the brokenhearted, to preach deliverance to the captives, and recovering of sight to the blind, to set at liberty them that are bruised, to preach the acceptable year of the Lord" (Luke 4:18–19).

Members that generated a list "must" accompany the trained member on all visitations. This is how we attempt to engage all members to fulfill the Great Commission. Instead of passing the name to someone else, they have to set the appointment and accompany visits to neighbors. The spirit of evangelism in a church is caught, not taught.

Pastors would encourage members to generate a list of all family members, neighbors, friends, loved-ones, and co-workers that are unsaved. We recommend that pastors hold the Set the Captives Free form up during Sunday service. The forms can be in the pews or placed in church bulletins. The forms should be collected and given to the prayer ministry for continued prayer. Along with the prayer ministry, church members would fast and pray as well, according to Isaiah 58, the fast God has chosen, "to loose the bands of wickedness, to undo the heavy burdens, and to let the oppressed go free (set the captives free). We should fast and pray to help others obtain freedom from sin.

"Set the Captives Free!" is a tactic for personal and blitz evangelism, undergirded by prayer. Church members pray and then intentionally share Christ with family, friends, and coworkers in personal evangelism. Trained members accompany untrained members on visitations to family, friends, coworkers, and neighbors. Training takes place as members assist in training untrained ones, helping to train them and igniting the spirit of evangelism. It is caught, not taught. Set the Captives Free strategy is designed to engage the entire congregation to fulfill the Great Commission. As members generate a list of unsaved family members, friends, loved-ones, neighbors, and co-workers; continued prayer and fasting are a must by members that will participate. Members that generated a list "must" accompany the trained member on all visitations. This is how we attempt to engage all members to fulfill the Great Commission. Instead of passing the name to someone else, they have to set the appointment or accompany visits to neighbors. The spirit of evangelism in a church is caught, not taught. Anytime during or after personal visitations, members will blitz or evangelize those with whom they share common interests, their neighbors. Members help members "possess their land" – their personal relationships and neighborhood.

Personal and Blitz With Others

List names of family members, friends, neighbors, and coworkers on the "Set the Captives Free!" prayer form. Make duplicate copies to distribute to the prayer ministry.

Pray:

- That the heavenly Father draws the lost (John 6:44). Only God can draw men to Himself.
- That the Holy Spirit convicts lost persons (John 16:8). A man will never see his sin unless the Holy Spirit reveals it to him. The Holy Spirit has to bring conviction of the sin.
- That God grants repentance to unbelievers (2 Tim. 2:25). God's goodness leads men to repent (Rom. 2:4).
- Pray for receptive hearts (Luke 8:5, 12). A lost person's heart needs to be broken to receive the seed of the gospel. Mark 4 reveals different types of ground. If the heart is hard, the soil is hard. If the heart is soft, the soil is fertile to give the lost person a receptive heart.
- That the lost person's eyes will be opened (Eph. 1:18–20). Although Paul was writing to believers, the truth of God opening eyes applies to the lost as well.

  For personal visitations, the person who generated the prayer list will call one person at a time to schedule a visit. If the member is not trained in evangelism techniques, a trained member will accompany the member on the visitation. For example: "Hello, this is _____, are you going to be home on _____? I was going to drop by and talk to you." (The prospect will think you need his advice.)

- Meet another trained member of your church or go by yourself to the home, praying before you go. Knock on the door, greet them, and introduce the person who is with you.

- Once inside the home, tell the family member, friend, neighbor, or coworker that your church has been praying for them and their family. "We came by tonight to say that we will continue to pray for you and your family, and that while we are here, if you have any prayer needs, with your permission we will pray."
- Listen for their response. If no response, tell them you will be leaving, but before you go, ask if you could pray with them.
- Give them an invitation to attend church, or share the gospel.

Blitz (Neighborhood Visitation)

Trained members accompany untrained members within their neighborhoods or apartment complex.

- Meet at member's home.
- Pray before you leave (refer to section on prayer).
- Proceed to neighbor's home and knock on door.
- When neighbor opens the door, the member should greet the neighbor and introduce the accompanying member.
- Member should explain that the church has been praying for the neighbors' family and stopped by today to personally pray for them and their family.
- A general prayer for the family, their needs, and God's blessing would be in order.
- After prayer, thank them and proceed to ask if they attend church in the area. If not, give them an invitation to visit your church. If they attend church in the area, ask if they are a church member or whether or not they have received Christ. If they are church members only, it is important to explain that church membership is not salvation. Ask for permission to share God's plan of salvation to them (see evangelism workshop section).
- If they refuse prayer, invite them to visit your church or share Christ with them. Thank them and leave.

Check List/Things Needed for Community Evangelism

- Have the Demographics Team spy the neighborhood.
- Pray over the area and the people.
- Train all participants in the Soul-Winning Evangelism Workshop.
- Prepare to go out and gather maps, tally forms, pens, clipboards and Bibles. I do not recommend taking large Bibles door-to-door. They raise preconceived notions and reduce people's willingness to talk to you. Have Bibles in your vehicles for

new converts who do not have their own. You can order affordable Bibles from the American Bible Society at www.bibles.com or 1-800-32-BIBLE.

- Divide into groups of no less than two people. I recommend three people in each group: one to witness, one to pray, and one to write.
- Reconvene for the groups to share their testimonies of their experiences and record attendance and results.
- Report results to the Communications Team and/or pastor.

Youth Strategy Brother-to-Brother

Brother-to-Brother is an afternoon of fun and fellowship with thirty minutes of Bible instruction for middle and high school students. It is by far the most successfully compelling method to draw young people because the children tell other children, and it grows quickly. Brother Milton and Sister Sheila Arnum, members of Greenforest Community Baptist Church, decided to put the vision of the Joshua Ministry into action. Sheila organized Brother-to-Brother, a group of men who spend time with boys from high crime areas once a month, having fun and sharing God's Word. The men are prosecutors, defense attorneys, ex-offenders, law enforcement officers, entrepreneurs, college students, teachers, foster parents, fathers of incarcerated men and boys, ministers and others. Their activities include go-carts, dunk tanks, volleyball, basketball, horse shoes, football, foosball, ping-pong, limbo stick, smoothie stand and more. At these monthly fellowships, the boys learn how to be men while they play, eat, sing, pray and study the Bible together. Successful business men and women come and give their stories which have resulted in career paths (college, flight school and other areas), as boys realize dreams and potential within. The boys are transported by bus from their neighborhoods to the fellowship location. The men meet and fellowship with each other from noon until 1:00 PM. When the boys arrive at 1:00 PM, the men greet them with love as they exit the buses. The event lasts until 5:00 PM. While Sheila's program is designed to reach at-risk boys who live in high crime areas, her concept can be used to effectively reach all middle school and high school students. You can call it whatever you like as long as it has the following components:

- Fellowship
- Fun
- Bible study (30 minutes maximum)
- Bible instruction is a must. If you do not include Bible study, then the gathering is just another day of fun. The Bible is what separates this event from similar secular activities.

The primary goal of Brother-to-Brother (or any similar program) is to draw middle and high school students to Christ.

Implementation

Follow these steps to implement a youth outreach program:
- Select a neighborhood.
- Pray over the selected area and the people.
- Determine needed resources: space, adult volunteers, money, food, games, Bibles, etc. Costs can be minimized by asking adults from the church to donate food items. If you are in a climate that gets cold during the winter months, find facilities for indoor activities. It is important the program does not shut down, but continues throughout the year.
- Identify other community resources and government agencies to support your program.
- Obtain legal permits, including parental consent and medical release forms, if necessary.
- Invite middle and high school students in the neighborhood to a fellowship event. This is your bait. Make it fun!
- Record attendance and results. (See Tracking Results under Implementation Process).
- Report results to the Communications Team and/or pastor.

Track Distribution

Gospel tracks have been around for years. Even though they have been around for years, they can be a very effective method for those who would leave. Hand someone a pamphlet as opposed to verbalizing the gospel.

Internet Evangelism

The Internet has opened a tremendous door for communicating. As I stated above, it has its place. However, we can encourage and share the gospel through email, Twitter, and Facebook, but we must not forsake the assembling (Hebrews10:25). The Internet can foster discussion and prayer but the command is that we go. The ministry of Jesus included listening but also touching, something we need not get away from.

Needs Based Evangelism

Something Jesus practiced. He met needs first and that gave Him the right to speak into the lives of those he ministered to. Churches have used this strategy for years, however, at some point we must communicate the gospel. People's souls are more important than their stomachs.

Guest Cards

Guest cards are simply business cards that have church information on them. Members can hand them out as they encounter people through daily activities. Simply hand them the card and give them an invitation to visit your church.

Multiplication by One

If everyone won one, and that one won one, think how many ones would be won. Everyone can invite or share Christ at some point. Most church growth today comes through members rotating, changing churches. Some church memberships are the same at the end of the year as they were at the beginning of the year. If everyone could invite or share Christ to just one person, the potential growth in one year could double.

Seed Casting

Seed casting is simply placing door hangers on doors in new subdivisions. We miss opportunities when new people move into our communities or new subdivisions are erected. Those who move from somewhere else need a church home somewhere.

Adopt-a-Neighborhood

Churches can select an apartment complex, neighborhood, or street, and cultivate the land. The church can create projects in the neighborhood, offer tutorial programs, senior citizen assistance or whatever. The goal is to make the church visible in the community and plant seeds for future harvest. In addition, it is to build a bridge between the church and community. The community will become heralds who will tell others what the church is doing to help the community.

Blitz

A blitz is simply going into a neighborhood or apartment complex and going door-by-door sharing the gospel and meeting needs. The blitzes can be carried out by your Sunday school classes. I recommend dividing the classes into tribes, and then sending the tribes out on a rotational basis. Tribal Leaders from the Evangelism Ministry coordinate each blitz. This provides an ongoing, systematic means of witnessing in your surrounding community. As each class returns from the blitz, the Assimilation Leader then contacts new converts and invites them to Sunday school and worship. The new converts grow spiritually and make other disciples.

Crusades

Take the ministry of the church to the streets. A crusade may be held
in a park or on a street corner. Examples are outdoor concerts and drama
(plays) on the street. The event should include a sermonette, a short message
of the gospel. Tracts and guest cards are distributed to the crowd. The goals of a crusade
are to:

- Share the gospel message and an invitation to accept Christ.
- Invite people to church.

Follow these steps to host a crusade:

- Partner with other ministries in the church to take the gospel to the streets.
- Pray to discern God's desire for the event. Also, pray for the people.
- Plan the event, identifying needed resources, e.g., equipment, materials, refreshments, etc.
- Obtain legal permission from local officials.
- Prepare forms to record the names and contact information of new converts.
- Conduct the crusade.
- Clean up the area afterward. Do not leave the site covered with trash. Give the contact information for the new converts to the Follow-Up Team.
- Record attendance and results.

Notes

PRINCIPLES OF SUCCESSFUL EVANGELISM

The Book of Joshua provides several principles for successful evangelism. Listed below are eight biblical principles for successful evangelism.

Spy the Land

"And Joshua the son of Nun sent out of Shittim two men to spy secretly, saying, Go view the land, even Jericho" (Joshua 2:1).

To "spy the land" means becoming aware of the demographics of the neighborhood. This includes the residents, their needs and the problems that plague their community. It also includes identifying other ministries and faith-based organizations within the community that residents can be referred for additional solutions.

Follow God's Direction

"And they commanded the people, saying, When ye see the ark of the covenant of the Lord your God, and the priest the Levites bearing it, then ye shall remove from your place, and go after it…for you have not passed this way heretofore" (Joshua 3:3–4).

God gave specific direction throughout the Book of Joshua as to how the Israelites were to possess the land. God may have a specific strategy to take the land and meet the needs of the community. I have found that God will lead you to the right person, who is receptive and has a real need for ministry at a specific time. If we are not directed by God, we can miss the move of God.

Sanctify Yourself

"And Joshua said unto the people; sanctify yourselves for tomorrow the Lord will do wonders among you" (Joshua 3:5).

To "sanctify" means to be set apart or set aside for God's service. It means that we allow God and His gifts to flow through us. This commitment must start with cleansing ourselves of any known sin in our lives. God will not be present in the battle or our efforts if sin is in the camp. When we sanctify ourselves, God will dwell with us and fight our battles.

Move Out in Faith

"And it shall come to pass, as soon as the soles of the feet of the priest that bear the ark of the Lord, the Lord of all the earth, shall rest in the waters of the Jordan, that the waters of Jordan shall be cut off from the waters that come down from above; and they shall stand upon an heap. And it came to pass as the people remove from their tents to pass over Jordan and the priest bearing the Ark of the Covenant before the people" (Joshua 3:13–14).

There must always be an element of faith. Without faith, we depend on our own ability, and God will not receive the proper glory due Him. It took faith for them to go where they had not been before. As long as the task seems overwhelming, the glory will be God's alone. When we realize our inability to accomplish what God has told us to do, we will then depend on His help. The Israelites stepped out on faith as God led the way. We must first move out in faith before God will manifest His power in our lives.

God Will Confirm His Presence

"And Joshua said, Hereby ye shall know that the living God is among you, and that He will without fail drive out from before you the Canaanites, and the Hittites, and the... (Joshua 3:10).

As long as the Israelites sanctified themselves and faith was present, God Manifested His power which resulted in victory. We will know God is with us when lives are changed. We will hear comments from those to whom we minister, confirming His presence among us. They will say things like, "I was just praying for God to send help."

God Will Give You a Testimony

"That this may be a sign among you, that when your children ask their fathers in time to come, saying, what mean ye these stones? Then ye shall answer them" (Joshua 4:6–7).

If we cleanse ourselves and move out in obedience, God will always do miraculous things we can share with others as a testimony of His presence and power. Testimonies will generate excitement for your ministry and lead others to Christ and the mission field.

Continue Campaign

"And the priest that bare the ark of the covenant of the Lord stood firm on dry ground in the midst of the Jordan, and all the Israelites passed over on dry ground, until all the people were passed clean over Jordan" (Joshua 3:17).

When the priest put their feet in the water, the Jordan River divided. As we get involved in people's lives and communities, we must continue our efforts. If not, their lives will return to their original state just as the water went back together when the priest removed their feet from the Jordan River. Our evangelism efforts must be a continuous campaign.

Give God the Glory

"Then Joshua built an altar unto the Lord God of Israel in mount Ebal" (Joshua 8:30). After victory at Ai, Joshua built an altar to the Lord who gave them the victory. We must never be guilty of stealing the glory that only belongs to God. We can never take credit for what He does in our midst. Be careful to praise only Him.

Notes

EVANGELISM STYLES

Darrell Robinson mentions in his book, *People Sharing Jesus*, that the apostle Paul tailored his presentation based on the individual's characteristics, culture, and background. Paul varied his approach based on the need of the person he was witnessing to. In Athens, he introduced them to the one that had built an altar: He went to the marketplace in Ephesus, from house to house, and used a direct approach to those in Corinth. Robinson says that there are varying levels as to how people can be encountered. He lists them in his book which I recommended.

Based on his premise, knowing different approaches will provide additional tools to the witness.

Intellectual

If you engage in a confrontational match with a Jehovah Witness, you would lessen the chance to reach him or her. Yet, if you shifted to an intellectual style you might progress further in your attempt to communicate the gospel. Jehovah Witnesses are intellectual people, so an intellectual style would yield greater results then being confrontational.

During his visit to Athens (Acts 17:16–34) Paul was stirred in his spirit based on residents' loyalty to idolatry. He disputed, or was confrontational in nature with them. This did not go over so good. However, when he was brought before Areopagus, he changed his style and became intellectual in nature. He caught their attention by mentioning their own poets.

Confrontation

There are times when confrontation may be a means to communicate the gospel. According to 2 Timothy 4:2, we are to reprove and rebuke at times.

In Acts 2, Peter used a confrontational approach to win converts during the day of Pentecost. Someone with this style is bold, and direct, and strong on their convictions.

Testimonial

This approach links one's own experiences with the one they witness to. Keep in mind, using your testimony means you may have to share personal information about your life.

In John 9, Jesus heals a man born blind. When asked how this was possible, He rehearsed the events just as they occurred. His rehearsal of the events was His testimony. Some will be won based on your testimony. We discussed our testimony and its components in an earlier session.

Interaction

A person using this approach is conversational, compassionate, focuses on the needs of others, and will build friendships. In Luke 5, Matthew used this approach after following Jesus. Through fellowship and relationships, people are won to Christ. Paul became all things to all men so he might win them.

> Though I am free and belong to no man, I make myself a slave to everyone, to win as many as possible. To the Jews, I became like a Jew, to win the Jews. To those under the law I became like one under the law (though I myself am not under the law), so as to win those under the law. To those not having the law I become like one not having the law (though I am not free from God's law but am under Christ's law), so as to win those not having the law. To the weak I became weak, to win the weak. I have become all things to all men so that by all possible means I might save some. I do all this for the sake of the gospel that I may share in its blessings (1 Corinthians 9:19–23).

The person that is conversational, compassionate, sensitive, and friendly will flourish using this approach.

Invitation

People that use this approach to win the lost will simply invite others to attend an event at church. However, you must at some point share the gospel.

The woman at the well used this approach in John 4. After an encounter with Jesus, she enters into the city and simply gives an invitation to others to experience a time with the Savior.

Serving

Do something for someone and they will feel like they owe you. At this point, you have their ear. You can talk about anything you want.

In Matthew 5:16, we are told to let our light shine that others will see God. There are two ways in which we shine our light. One is the way in which we live; the other is the way we serve others.

Notes

CULTS AND OTHER RELIGIONS

There is a battle over the lost souls of men. Although our spiritual warfare efforts are directed towards Satan releasing those held in bondage of sin, that sin seems to be more entrenched in those who are enamored and deceived by beliefs in a false man-made theology with no real assurance of salvation. So are most cults and other religions.

In this section we want to convey beliefs and practices of some, not all, cults and other religions. It is my intent to familiarize you with the the cults and religions you are most likely to encounter.

I have identified some common areas that cults and other religions share: (1) They are united in their faith. (2) They have a strong teaching base. (3) All members propagate a united message. (4) They have an allegiance to the founder. (5) They place strong emphasis on training their children. (6) They oppose Christians and their message. (7) They are strong in beliefs and practices.

At the end of this session I will list some things we can do as Christians to strengthen our witness to non-Christian groups.

Buddhism

Most Buddhists believe in Buddha and believe he is an enlightened teacher or God. They do not believe in Jesus and that he died a substitutionary atonement for the sins of the world. They do not regard the Bible as an authoritative source. To escape suffering, one needs to follow the sacred, Noble Eightfold Path: right views, aspiration, speech, conduct, livelihood, effort, mindfulness, and concentration.

Mormons

Mormons were founded by Joseph Smith who claimed the angel Morona appeared to him. He also claims Jesus appeared to him and told him all other churches were wrong and had fallen into apostate. He was to restore true Christianity. The origin of their organization is man-made, not originated by Jesus Christ. Most Mormons consider themselves as Christians. They use common words to communicate their beliefs. By this, they appear to be Christians but are not. They consider themselves as the one true church. Mormons believe the Bible is corrupt and do not regard it as authoritative. They use the Bible, but only hold to its interpretation as Joseph Smith, the founder, interprets it. Mormons have three other sources they use as well: *The Book of Mormons*, *The Doctrine of Covenants*, and *The Pearl of Great Price*. The common points Christians and Mormons share are morality and family.

Hinduism

Most Hindus believe and accept any God. They know little about Jesus and regard Him as a spiritual master or teacher. They do not believe He died a substitutionary death. They are not familiar with the Bible and have their own books including the *Vedas, Upanisbas*, and *Bbagavad Gita*. We should first build relationships.

Islam

Muslims regard Jesus as a prophet. They believe the prophet Muhammad was the final prophet. Muslim's holy book called the Qur'an, is regarded as superior to the Bible.

Muslims believe that salvation is obtained by being a faithful Muslim, and by practicing five pillars of faith, living a morally upright life, and obeying Allah's (God's) commands as taught in the Qur'an.

The Shahada, or "confession" is declared by Muslims all over the world. It states, "here is not God but Allah, and Muhammad is the prophet (or messenger).

Islam is one of the largest religions in the world along with Christianity, Judaism, and Hinduism. The name came out of the revelations and teachings of its founder Muhammad, and is the Arabic term for "submission."

The Qur'an is the holy book Muslims adhere to. Muslims believe the Bible cannot be trusted because it has been interpreted by men and that God directly gave His revelation to Muhammad.

Every Muslim who hopes to escape the judgment of Allah must fulfill five pillars of faith (Sura 10:109):

1. Recitation of the Shahada (There is no God but Allah, and Muhammad is the prophet of Allah).

2. Pray five times a day (Salat or Namaz) facing Mecca.

3. Give one-fourth of their income as a charitable contribution (Almsgiving - Zakat).

4. Fast (Saum or Ruzeh) during the entire month of Ramadan. Muslims are to fast from all food and drink from sunrise to sunset in atonement for their own sins.

5. A pilgrimage (Hajj) to Mecca, the holy city, at least once in a Muslim's life. Holy War (gihad) used to be a condition of faith. Some Muslims believe it is their sacred duty to murder anyone that does not embrace the one true faith.

The Nation of Islam

The Nation of Islam derives from a group called the Moorish-American Science Temple in Newark, New Jersey, established in 1913 by B. Timothy Drew. Drew changed his name to Noble Drew Ali and claimed he had received a commission from the king of Morocco to spread Islam in the United States. After Drew's death, Wallace D. Farad, who changed his name to Wallace Frad Muhammad, claimed to have been born in Mecca in 1877 and became leader. Fard left the Nation after being arrested and Elijah Muhammad took over the rein. His sons who changed the Nation to a form of orthodox Islam followed him. In 1977, the Honorable Louis Abdul Farrakhan broke away from the Nation and returned to the original name and beliefs, which are radical and racist in nature, and believe that Christianity is the white man's religion.

Jehovah's Witnesses

A governing body of elders that exercise authority on all doctrinal matters directs Jehovah's Witnesses. Witnesses base their beliefs on the Bible, and prefer their own literal, conservative translation, the *New World Translation of the Holy Scriptures.*

The group emerged from the Bible Student movement, founded in the late 19th century by Charles Taze Russell, with the formation of Zion's Watch Tower Tract Society. Following a schism in the movement, the branch that maintained control of the Society underwent significant organizational changes, bringing its authority structure and methods of evangelism under centralized control. The name *Jehovah's Witnesses*, based on Isaiah 43:10–12, was adopted in 1931.

Since its inception, the Watch Tower Society has taught that the present world order is in its last days and will soon be destroyed at Armageddon. It has stated that only Jehovah's Witnesses "have any Scriptural hope of surviving the impending end of this doomed system," but that God decides who will survive. Those whom God chooses to save—survivors and resurrected individuals—will have the opportunity to live forever in an earthly paradise, ruled by Christ and 144,000 humans raised to heaven.

New Age

New Age movement is somewhat obscured. There is not a specific founder, leader, headquarters, organizational structure, or beliefs. Basically, it is a large network of organizations and individuals who share common values, based on mysticism and monoism – the worldview that "all is one"

God, to the New Age movement is not the same personage we defined. Rather they define "God" as an impersonal force pervading all creation. Basically, they have rejected the Christian doctrine of man's need for salvation.

How Do We Reach Them?

As Christians, we should do all we can to reach those held in bondage and deception. They are not the enemy because they are in bondage. Love never fails and it's through love that others are drawn to Him.

I believe there are some things we can learn from some of these groups that can help in our process to reach them.

- Pray for them.
- Become strong in our faith and practice. It is obvious that most cults and religions are strong in both faith and practice. Hypocrisy has long been a hindering factor in Christian evangelism.
- Build relationships – we will never progress past walls of resistance without first building relationships. Are we afraid of dialog?

Are we afraid something they believe is going to rub off on us? Have we sinned if we converse with them or are seen in the same geographic location as some of them?

- The common ground we share with most groups can be found in the area of morality.
- Get acquainted with points of belief, especially major points of belief and eternal life.
- Become familiar with their customs, cultures, and traditions.
- Look for common points with Christianity.
- Remember God is the great evangelist who draws the lost and the Holy Spirit will convict and reveal Jesus to them.
- Meet a natural need; you will have a listening ear.
- Don't argue.

Talking Points

I was talking with a friend that suggested we take what he called "talking points," used by Jehovah's Witnesses and use them to open conversations. He said when Jehovah's Witnesses come to your door they gain interest by using "talking points." Talking points are relative points of interest that are used to draw people into conversation which will lead to a potential convert. For example, when focusing on teens, they would present a booklet with teens on the cover, with its contents posing questions and solutions to relevant problems in society. The table of contents draws one to explore beyond the cover to discover relief from life's struggles. Materials can be developed for each age group, peoples group, or subculture.

The following is a brief testimony from a student at the university where I teach Urban Evangelism. Students were given an assignment to interview someone from another race other than their own to ascertain what would cause them to consider attending your church or the Christian faith.

I have a couple in my church that comes from India. The wife is a confessing Hindu. Their daughter has a semi crippling disease called spinal bifida. They were encouraged by a family member to bring the daughter to a service and allow me to pray for her. They came forward at the end of the service when I called for those who needed prayer for spiritual or physical healing. The Hindu mother was in tears. I prayed for her and her daughter. When she explained the surgical procedure that the girl was to go through I made the decision to be with them through the 12 hour surgery.

While the daughter was going through the surgery I began to ask the mother questions about her faith and her understanding of Jesus Christ. Though she acknowledged Christ, it wasn't with the same status which Christianity places Him. I chose at that moment not to push her to a deeper acknowledgement. It just seemed that this was how the Spirit of God was unctioning me to react.

I spent much of that day and subsequent days with the family in visitation. The daughter came through the surgery with amazing results. I always prayed for her with the parents there. They would bow their heads with me as I would call on God to do miraculous things. I would pray for their faith as well.

This family is in regular attendance with me at church. They acknowledge Christ as Lord and are growing more and more in Him. To this day, I don't remember pressing them, especially the mother, to receive Christ as Lord and Savior but it is apparent that something is drawing them.

Since the surgery, more than a year ago, they are attending church, worshipping Christ, and coming to the altar as they feel led. It amazes me to see. I will eventually inquire as to their faith in Jesus more specifically. I was brought to the Scripture where Paul approached the people on Mars Hill who were paying respects to a multitude of spiritual entities, the moon god, the sun god etc., and how Paul, rather than put down the objects of the other gods, noticed the one icon that acknowledged the "unknown god." Here he began to tell them about Christ, telling them that He was the unknown God (to them). It is a marvelous thing to see this unfold before me. I have determined to love these people and see how God will reveal Himself to them through the days and months to come.

This testimony should cause all of us to praise God and give us faith in what He alone can do to win any person to Himself. We must rely on His power and use information to support us as we seek to lead others to Christ.

Some common traits among some of these groups are listed below:
- They are united in strong faith.
- They promote strong teaching among all members.
- They propagate one unified message.
- They are willing to die for their god or leader.
- They place strong emphases on teaching children.
- They oppose the Christian message.
- They have a strong belief and practice.

A Few More Things

The following are some terms that will aide in our quest to understand the beliefs of others.
- **Agnosticism:** there are two basic kinds of agnostics: those who claim that the existence and nature of God are not known, and those who hold God to be unknowable.
- **Atheism:** claim there is no God.
- **Rationlism:** hold that what is knowable or demonstrable by human reason is true. Therefore, the existence of God can be demonstrated with logical necessity.
- **Pragmatism:** the belief that one cannot think or feel truth, but can discover it by attempting to live it.
- **Deism:** the belief that there is a God both beyond and within the world, a Creator and Sustainer who sovereignly controls the world but denies his supernatural intervention in it on the grounds that the world operates by natural and self-sustaining laws of the Creator.
- **Pantheism:** believes that God is beyond the world but not in it. God is the world.

The brief material above is by no means an exhausted list or teaching of this subject matter. I strongly suggest a course in Christian Apologetics to gain further education on cults and religion.

Notes

Notes

HOW TO REACH YOUTH

I started to begin this chapter by saying that youth are the most challenging group we encounter. However, to say this I would be lessening the power of God to deliver. God is still God and his Word still true.

Our youth are merely a sub-culture among us. A sub-culture is a group that holds to a set of governing principles that are not embraced by the dominate culture. Gangs in particular, do not feel they fit into the majority culture and have found within themselves a separate society.

Based on our experience both on the streets and working with Brother-to- Brother, which we discussed in the strategy section, the following are what we have seen work:

- Fast and pray according to instructions in the chapter on prayer.
- Know that it takes time to raise a crop.
- It is important to plant seed in children.
- Develop a relationship – most of us seem to minister from a distance fishing from the bank or throwing money into the water. The strategy used by Brother-to-Brother at Greenforest involves getting into the water.
- Spend quality time with youth.
- Listen to them.
- Love, accept, value them, and know they have worth. Love them with the love of God, accept them where they are in life, value them as God's creation, and know that within them there is worth; something God has placed in each one of them for His purpose on this earth.

Points to Consider

As I stated in an earlier chapter, to know the customs, culture, and traditions will go a long way in finding points of entry or common ground to begin to build relationships.

- Do not live one way on Sunday and another way at home. I believe our biggest harvest among youth will be directly attributed to our crying out to God through fasting and prayer, putting away our hypocrisy, and becoming relationally involved with them.
- Youth are loyal.

- Youth are community driven.
- Youth are service-minded.
- Youth accept other races.
- Youth are concerned about political, social, and economy.
- Youth are spiritual but not religious.

Around the Table

I believe the most simplistic relational tool we have lost in our society is what families used to do around the table. Family time around meals solidified love, acceptance, and security needed by youth. Our absence from the table has been replaced by local gangs who are willing to supply the security that the table brings.

Statistics

I thought about supplying statistics but we all know what is going on in our society. How to make an inroad into the statistics is the challenge. Let's start by laboring in prayer and allowing God to do the work in them. He can, and will, draw them. Let's not give up on them.

In Joshua 4:6, the children of Israel were to communicate to their children how God had brought them across the Jordan River. In the same manner, we must accept the responsibility of sharing how God's great power of deliverance took us out of the bondage of sin. By sharing our experience with others, the door will then be opened for us to share how God can change their lives. It would also teach them how they can communicate the Gospel to their peers one generation to the next communicating what God has done. The Joshua Generation: God's Witnessing Army, are the teenagers, those the world has labeled Generation X, but who we believe are going to be greatly used by God. They're not worthless as some would say, but they are of great value in God's army. This group has the potential to be a witnessing army with the same spirit and courage that Joshua exhibited. It was during a teen conference at Greenforest Community Baptist Church in 1999 that the tract entitled Teen Evangelism was added. During this effort, fifteen souls received Jesus Christ for the first time. Teens get very excited when God uses them to make a difference in another teenager's life. I find that teens are very relational and are concerned about the problems of other teens. Excitement and concern are two areas that motivate teens to minister to others. It almost seems to be an impossible task to win our own children and other teens to Christ. However, I would like to share what we did in our own home when one of our children came under attack by the enemy, and then share a complete evangelism program for teens. At the age of fifteen, our middle son D'Juan, didn't want anything to do with God or the church. I don't need to go into a lot of details concerning what happened; however, those who have had a teen rebel against God understand what it is like for the parents going through such a phase/ordeal. This is what God led us to do and how He brought victory into our home within a few months.

In God's Word I found principles that I could use to bring tremendous change within my own family. The principles are found in Mark 5:21–24 and Mark 7. In Mark 5, we have the story of Jairus who came to Jesus because his daughter was sick and later died. In Mark 7, we have the story of the Syrophenician woman who wanted Jesus to cast an unclean spirit out of her daughter. In both stories there were three principles that were used, and as a result, the parent received the child back. The first thing is they had faith; even when the condition became worse they still believed God. Sometimes when we pray and we see things get worse, we take it out of God's hand; however, we should fall down and worship Jesus. Notice, they didn't complain or get an attitude towards God or ask why, they simply praised Him. God's Word admonishes us to give God praise in all things, not for the situation, but in the midst of the situation. The third thing the parents did was they besought Him, they asked Him, and made a request unto Him to get involved. What is God saying? What does God want to do? How does He want to do it? When we have problems we tend to tell God what to do and how to do it, when instead we should find out His will and purpose for the situation.

In 1 Kings 17:17–22, there is another principle. Here we find Elijah who took a dead boy and laid him across his bed, cried unto the Lord, and stretched himself upon the child three times. As he cried to God, the child's spirit returned unto him again. This principle teaches us that sometimes we need to get down, lay prostrate before the Lord, and as I say, just get a hold of the altar until God moves. We must have patience. God will move in our teens' lives if we use these principles found in His Word. They worked in my family.

Teens want to belong to and identify with something. For whatever reason, the lack of family interaction in the home has caused our teens to look elsewhere for a real sense of belonging. Hence, the gang, in too many cases, fits the bill. This generation is the first generation in history predicated to do worse than their parents did. Our society has already concluded that they are not going to amount to anything, and has marked them. We have marked them X, a generation with no hope. However, The Joshua Generation: God's Witnessing Army concept gives teens a sense of identity and purpose that they are searching for. I believe God has great things in store for this group. As I talk to teens, I have found that they are very hungry. The hunger is for something real. However, as they look at the church at large, they say they haven't seen anything that's real. Teens say church people are hypocritical because they say one thing and do another. If the church could demonstrate Him, teens would be drawn to Him. The singing and shouting we do does not demonstrate to them a living Christ when we live a different lifestyle at home. In most cases, teens can sing and shout circles around us. To reach them, we're not talking about changing God's Word, but using the principles of God's unchanging Word. It does not change. It worked yesterday and it works today. The hunger our youth have can be a starting point to meet our youth where they are. Then we can introduce them to Christ and give them a true sense of belonging.

Once a teen has given his or her life to Christ, he/she will have a real sense of concern for his other peers. Teens want their friends to receive the same living Christ they have received. I don't know if we noticed it or not, but in the wake of the school shootings, the first place kids turned to was the church! They do believe in spiritual things and want to be connected to spiritual things. We must show them the way to a true and living Christ. I believe God is going to use this so-called Generation X and beyond in a great way. The church seems to be full of fear and will not cross over to possess the land God has already given to her. While most of us remain chained to our pews, this is a fearless generation that knows no limits and loves to take risks. God can use these characteristics in a great way. I have found that once teens form a relationship with Christ, they are on fire and want to win the world. I have seen them go into their schools with boldness and witness to their friends. They are not afraid to tell their friends about the love of Christ or to confront the sin in their friend's lives. They don't care where they share Christ. I believe that as adults, if we don't move out of our comfort zones, God is going to raise them up to do what we refuse to do. Like Joshua, they don't fear and don't mind stepping out, while most of us struggle in these areas.

In Joshua 5:7, we are told that God raised up their children in their stead. If teens can belong to Satan's gang, then why not God's army? Let's not X them out like the world, but pray that God may use them to move out towards others.

Teen Evangelism

Our youth are confronted with a world of problems, including drugs, teen pregnancy, suicide, confusion, gangs, violence, dysfunctional families, and other stressful things. However, there are several common denominators that I have noticed within all teens, that when properly understood and directed, become common factors and points of ministry, or can serve as the release of ministry. Most teens seem to struggle with acceptance, identity, and purpose. While at the same time, they are concerned for the misfortune of others and the condition of the world. I believe one of the causes of the rebellion among our teens is that they are reaching out for love and acceptance. However, gangs are not a real place for love and acceptance. The love and acceptance that gangs offer is distorted. It leaves no real solution for a world full of real problems.

My own teenage children, and hundreds of others at the high school and college level, are consistently involved in community projects. One of the ministries at Greenforest is a ministry that feeds the homeless every Saturday. I have noticed a large youth presence in this ministry. These teens do not have to be here, but they willingly volunteer their service. I have also noticed that every week when the Feed the Homeless Ministry meets, it's not always the same group of teens volunteering. They are concerned about certain conditions in our society. This concern for the less fortunate and world affairs are a good place to get them involved in ministry. Their concern for world events and the plight of others who are less fortunate identify points of passion and ministry within their group. When teens are released to work in these areas, it will bring fulfillment and direct them to a purpose for their lives. We can ascertain from these events that they look for purpose, acceptance, and fulfillment. Purpose and fulfillment can only be found in a relationship with Jesus Christ. Once we enter into a real relationship with Him, we will then understand that we are accepted in the beloved (Ephesians 1:6). With purpose and fulfillment as a base, the following Gospel presentation was developed for teens.

When I witness to teens, starting my presentation with an opening statement: God has a purpose for your life, without exception, the teens look at me with a puzzled or questioning look on their faces. This indicates that they are looking for purpose, thus opening the door to talk to them about the void God has put within the hearts of all men. Purpose and the void are what they are really seeking to discover.

The following is an outline of the Gospel presentation:

Introduction

Teens have their own dialogue. With that in mind, it's my suggestion to allow them to engage in their own normal conversation. From this point, the following diagnostic question can be asked so one can begin to talk to them about spiritual matters.

Diagnostic Question

List some of the things you and your friends do together, such as activities, places visited, and even bad things or habits done together (i.e., movies, smoking). Then ask them this question: Do you still feel like something is missing, or do you still feel unfulfilled? If they answer yes, say...

Witness: I feel the same way. Can I share with you what I have discovered? Wait for a response.

Witness: That unfulfilled feeling we have inside is a void that God has put in all of us. Now, I don't know how you feel about God or church, but let me share with you what I found out. When God created us, He placed within all of us a void that leads us down a road trying to find acceptance, purpose, and fulfillment for our lives. We're trying to fill a void that can only be satisfied when we accept Jesus and His plan for our life.

Transition

Do you ever think about spiritual things? Did you know God has a purpose for your life? Or say, do you want that hunger on the inside to be satisfied?

I. God wants us to have:
   a. A successful life now (John 10:10).
   b. Eternal life (John 3:16).

Eternal life is a free gift (Rom. 6:23). Have you received God's free gift of eternal life?

Transition

The reason the void is in our life is because of sin.

II. Sin is a universal problem.
   a. All have sinned (Rom. 3:23)
   b. God has to judge sin (Rom. 6:23a)

Transition

The only way we can solve the sin problem, fill the void, and find real purpose in life is to come into a relationship with Jesus Christ. The way we do this is to:

III. Repent
   a. Repent ye therefore, and be converted, that your sins may be blotted out Acts 3:19). To repent means to live a different lifestyle than we do now.
   b. Sin has to be judged. The payment for sin is death, but God s free gift to us is eternal life through Jesus Christ (Rom. 6:23).

IV. Accept and place our faith in what God has done through Jesus.
    a. God became flesh in the person of Jesus Christ (John 1:14)
    b. God placed our sin on Him (Isaiah 53:6; 1 Peter 3:18)
    c. By grace are we saved by faith (Ephesians 2:8)
    d. For those who accept Him, He gives the right to become His son (John 1:12)

V. Surrender our life to Jesus
    a. Confess with our mouth and believe in our heart (Romans 10:9–10)
    b. He saves us even though we don't deserve to be saved, by only trusting in Him. Salvation is a free gift from Him (Ephesians 2:8)
    c. Confess publicly/pray openly (Matthew 10:23, 33)

VI. Prayer of Commitment

> Dear heavenly Father, I am a sinner, but I heard the good news today that Jesus died for my sins. I ask you to forgive me for all of my sins. I believe in my heart, and confess with my mouth that Jesus died on the cross for my sins and was raised from the dead, and right now, I accept Him and receive Him as my Lord and Savior.

There are four things that sinners need to include while praying this prayer. First, there must be an acknowledgement of their sin(s). Second, they must ask for forgiveness of their sin. Third, they must believe that Jesus died for their sin. And fourth, they must accept Jesus into their life by faith according to Romans 10:9–10. The Scriptures above can be spoken in a manner that teens can better understand, perhaps if spoken in their own vernacular. We have to remember that this is not the sixteenth century, and the King James English is not the language we use today. The following Scriptures can be used to bring assurance to those who accept Christ.

VII. Assurance of salvation Scriptures
    a. He that believes on Christ has eternal life (John 6:47).
    b. I give unto them eternal life (John 10:28).

Personal Testimony

Another way teens can share the Gospel is by sharing their testimony. The personal testimony is one of the strongest tools we have. People can dispute the Bible all day long, but one's personal experience is factual. In Acts 26, Paul gives his personal testimony before King Agrippa. His testimony consisted of three parts: his life before Christ, his salvation experience, and his life since receiving Christ.

On the following page, write your personal testimony. Bo Mitchell, a teacher and great soul winner in the body of Christ, suggests starting your testimony by asking, "May I share with you the most exciting thing that happened to me?" In addition, he suggests ending your testimony by asking, "Has anything like this ever happened to you?"

Before Christ

_____

_____

_____

_____

_____

_____

Salvation Experience

_____

_____

_____

_____

_____

_____

Since Christ

_____

_____

_____

_____

_____

_____

Let's not miss the opportunity to share our own personal testimony with our children, and then teach them to share their story with others, especially their peers.

Note

EVANGELISM PRACTICUM

This session will focus on what students have learned in the classroom. Students will pair into groups and enter the fields of harvest. After a brief time in the community, students will return to class and discuss their experience. As an assignment, students will write their experience. Items needed are:

- Clip boards and pens
- Information forms
- Gospel track

Implementation Steps

- Pair off into teams of two or three.
- Assign one person to record, one to pray, and one to share.
- If the team is two members, one prays and records, and the other shares.
- Provide information to leave at the residence, including one sheet with information about your church. The information should be something the church has or is doing that would create an interest. Something that would meet a need or help develop the person.
- Provide maps with location and assigned streets.
- Provide prayer cards.
- Something to give, ranging from an ink pen to a light bulb. Some churches give light bulbs and say, "Jesus is the light of the world."
- Provide transportation, which could mean one vehicle or carpool
- Pray before you leave.

The time you spend in the community should be determined by the leader. Of course, if fish are biting, you would probably spend more time fishing. It is always exciting to see members that were full of apprehension set ablaze by their experience. In over 30 years doing this, I have never experienced a negative testimony. Satan blinds us to receive Christ and to share Christ. The same way people say, "I wish I had gotten saved years before," say, "Why haven't we done this before – share Christ to the lost?"

The map on the following page is of an apartment complex. A subdivision map can also be obtained or drawn. The purpose is to assign teams a specific building or street with to go door-to-door, praying, sharing Christ and meeting needs.

You can go to Yahoo, Microsoft, Kingdom Combine or any other software company and purchase programs that will assist in mapping your local area. Mark the church as your starting and the target location as your destination. When several teams are involved, we suggest the following:

- Designate a team leader.
- Number maps according to the number teams participating.
- Highlight the route to the location.
- Highlight an individual street for each team to work. We suggest two no more than three.
- One writes information and prays while the other shares.
- One team work one side of the street while another team works the other side. This allows each to observe the other.
- When at the door introduce yourself and that you are from _____ church.
- Follow instructions from the "Set the Captives Free" strategy. As an alterrnative method, you can use a survey, or say you have come by to meet our neighbors, if they are in the area of your church.
- Pray before you go out. Pray that God will forgive all sins of those participating.
- Pray for the lost and for the safety of the believer.

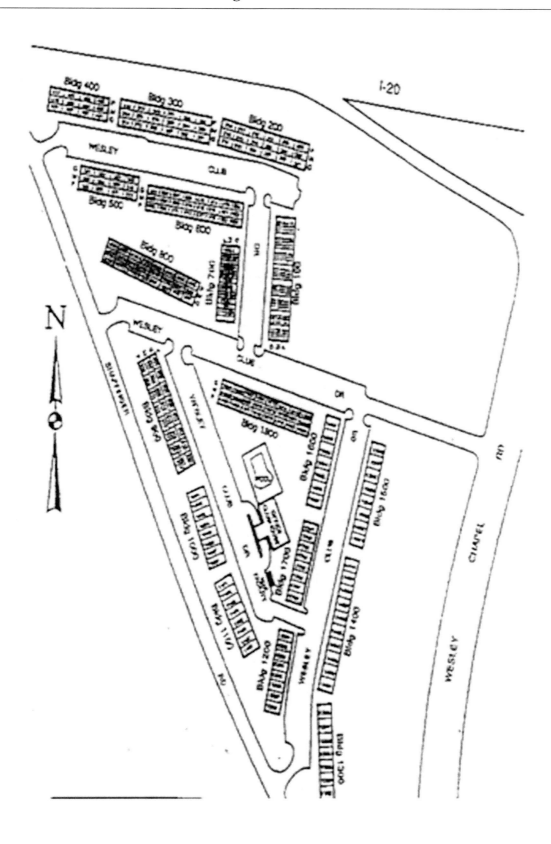

Notes

STRATEGY DEVELOPMENT

I n this chapter, the student is to take the provided information and develop an outreach strategy for their church. Students can incorporate strategies in earlier chapters. Use the following outline to develop a strategy.

1. Look up demographics for your area

2. Vision

3. Mission

4. Target people group
   - Youth
   - Teens
   - Children
   - Adults
   - Men
   - Women
   - Homeless
   - Nursing Homes
   - Guy Community
   - Inner City
   - Subdivision

5. Strategy

6. Action Steps

7. Assignments

8. Resources Needed

9. Follow up

10. Prayer

Other Resources by Dr. David Hopewell, Sr.

BOOKS

The Joshua Ministry, an evangelical strategy based in principle on the book of Joshua
Key to Becoming an Effective Associate Minister & Church Leader
Joshua Implementation Manual
Unity, The Highest Form of Evangelism
Set the Captives Free
Associate Minister & Church Leadership Training Manual

SCHOOLS

The Joshua Ministry School of Evangelism
The Joshua Ministry School of Associate Minister Training

ADDITIONAL INFORMATION

www.joshuaministry.com
Email: dhopewellsr@joshuaministry.net

LaVergne, TN USA
24 October 2010
201946LV00001B/11/P